This book is dedicated to my
family – my father Mohamed,
my mother Injoung and
my sister Eman.

————

*The heart is cooking a pot
of food for you. Be patient
until it is cooked.*
RUMI

✳✳✳

Amina is very proud of her Korean (from her mum) and Egyptian (from her dad) heritage. She and her sister, Eman, were born in Saudi Arabia but the family moved to Australia when Amina was four, and she has lived here ever since. Growing up in a household of two different cultures, she has always enjoyed cooking and eating both Korean and Middle Eastern dishes and she loves to share them with her family and friends.

In 2012, Amina was a contestant on *MasterChef Australia*, finishing in the top twelve, and endearing herself to all who saw her with her warmth and generosity – she has been described as 'everyone's best friend'. This was a wonderful opportunity for her to pursue her cooking career and also to bring Korean and Egyptian cooking to national attention.

Amina has written a monthly column for the *Australian Women's Weekly* and been a guest demonstrator at food events and shows in Australia and internationally. She also runs cooking classes, does corporate and private catering, helps to organise pop-up restaurants in Sydney and has just launched a halal food app called *Amina's Kitchen*.

In addition to cooking, she continues to work as a paediatric nurse at the Sydney Children's Hospitals Network, where she has been for the last seven years. That remains a much-loved career.

Amina has her own website, 'Amina's Alchemy', at aminasalchemy.com.

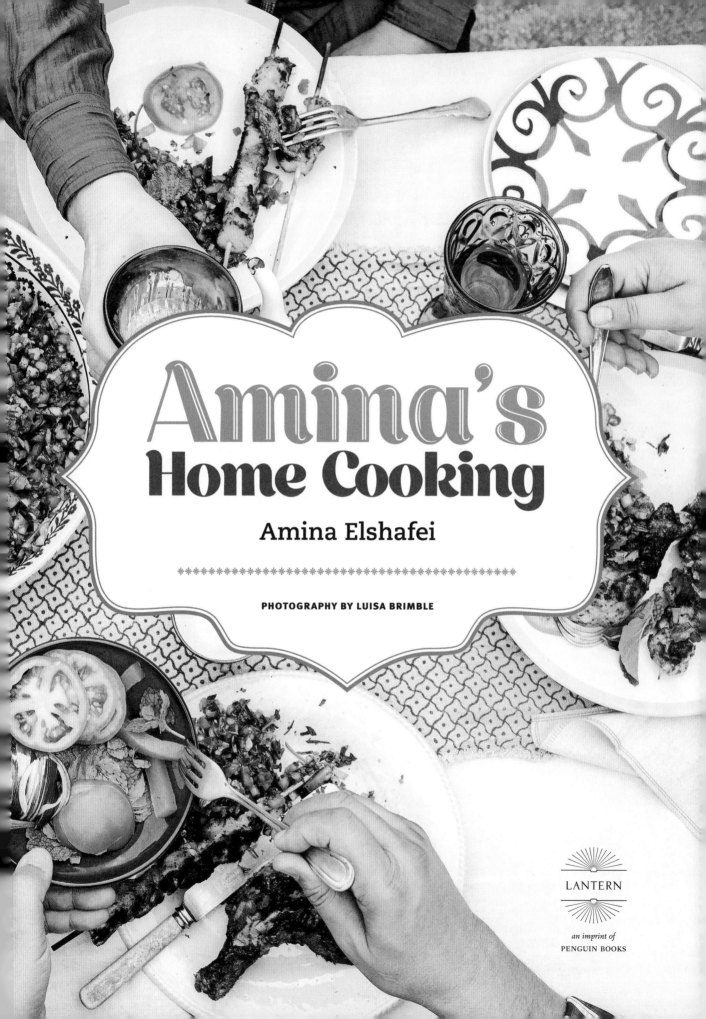

Amina's
Home Cooking

Amina Elshafei

****

PHOTOGRAPHY BY LUISA BRIMBLE

LANTERN

an imprint of
PENGUIN BOOKS

*

Foreword vii

Introduction 1

Middle Eastern pantry 7

Korean pantry 11

Starters 15

Vegetables, legumes and grains 55

Seafood 87

Poultry 117

Meat 147

Desserts 173

Middle Eastern suppliers 198

Korean suppliers 199

Acknowledgements 201

Index 203

*

Foreword

by Eman Elshafei

Nearly twenty years ago I sat down to my first koshari and kimchi dinner – a typical Elshafei meal, reflecting Dad and Mum's Egyptian and Korean heritage. I am now struck by the novelty of my family's cooking at the time, and by the transformation in the Australian food scene over the last two decades. There has been an evolution from the monocultural food of the 1980s to the wide range of national and specialty dishes now available – evidence of the impact people have on food.

This impact is integral to Amina's cooking – and part of the reason for her rising popularity. Exploring and mastering the foods of different countries has always been easy for her – we were spoilt by the cosmopolitan, multicultural atmosphere in which we grew up.

Of course, being blessed culturally explains only half the story of Amina's success. Equipped with a finely honed pan-Asian/Middle-Eastern palate, she was always a talented cook. I recall standing in the kitchen with her most Saturday evenings as she cooked – it was like being caught in a cross between *Iron Chef* and some Eastern Food Bazaar twilight zone, with the smells of samak and spices, sahlab and sikhye, soy sauce and soy bean blending with the sweet perfume of the orange blossom tree in our garden.

I love the way my sister's cooking always left us feeling comforted and reassured, thanks to her determination to create dishes that not only appealed to our tastebuds, but also contributed to our overall contentment. This is what has always made Amina's food especially priceless.

My sister's cooking reveals her absolute reverence for Korean and Middle Eastern wisdom, and the longstanding belief in both cultures in the importance of food for your physical and emotional wellbeing.

Shining even more brightly from the bottom of her cooking pan is her limitless generosity, her bubbly personality and her culinary skill, which always makes me come back for more.

Love,
Eman

DAD AND MUM.

DAD WITH EMAN AND ME
ON A SYDNEY FERRY.

WEARING MY *HANBOK*
(CEREMONIAL DRESS)
AT MY FIRST BIRTHDAY.

MY PATERNAL GRANDFATHER.

Introduction

Growing up, I learnt one important lesson in life at the dining table – never to underestimate the importance of food in life. I am very blessed to have been brought up in a household where sharing food is never considered just as a means of sustaining life, but rather as an enjoyable experience that continues to create more stories.

My parents were working in Saudi Arabia when they met. Mum was a nurse from Korea and Dad was an accountant from Egypt. After they'd married and had two daughters, first me and then my sister Eman, they decided to start a new life in Australia. They arrived here in 1989 with very little family or social support, ready to start the dream life, full of opportunities, in Sydney.

Living in a foreign country, they found the daily discoveries of new social and cultural customs quite challenging at times. One particular challenge was how to get access to the ingredients they needed for their Korean and Egyptian dishes. Even if they were able to find the right ingredients, those ingredients were not always fresh and could be quite expensive. However, if there was one aspect of life that my parents held onto quite closely, it was cooking and eating the food they grew up with. Even today, my mother and father continue to cook the wonderful dishes that remind them of their homelands, and sometimes they tell us stories linked to the dishes they cook.

As children, Eman and I would sit on the kitchen bench watching my parents cook and assisting with the tedious jobs, such as peeling garlic and onions or trimming beans. Observing my parents in the kitchen helped me to understand the different stages of cooking and the preparation techniques that I now feel so grateful to have learnt.

I began to cook with more interest (and perhaps seriousness) halfway through high school. I loved experimenting with food, and it was a great way to get out of studying. I remember trying to make a 'microwaveable' cake when I was about fourteen – I somehow managed to blow up the microwave, and the cake was inedible.

By the time I was at university, cooking was a must for me and a means of helping my parents, as they both worked full-time. It was one household chore that I really enjoyed! I was able to replicate some traditional Korean and Egyptian dishes at that point, and was also interested in learning about food from other cultures, including Italian, Chinese and Japanese food in particular.

The greatest change that I have seen in relation to cooking our cultural food is that access to both Korean and Middle Eastern ingredients has increased tremendously throughout Australia. The ingredients are now so fresh and abundant that it has become much easier to produce Korean and Middle Eastern food that is true to the traditional flavours and textures. I have included a list of Middle Eastern and Korean food suppliers on pages 198–199.

I think that Korean food is the most unique of all the Asian cuisines (not that I'm biased!). Its emphasis on fermentation, on consuming ingredients that are as fresh as possible and its incredible flavours make this cuisine really stand out. The fermentation technique used to make dishes such as kimchi was traditionally adopted to provide families with a choice of side dishes, called *bancham*, to accompany meals during the colder parts of the year when the frost and snow made it difficult to harvest fresh produce.

Korean food varies slightly throughout the different regions, but it is generally based on three elementary ingredients – chilli, soy sauce and sesame oil. These three ingredients when combined produce an incredible, distinct flavour, especially with slowly braised proteins. The other distinctive feature of Korean cuisine is how a meal is served. For all three meals, rice is plated in a small bowl, accompanied by a type of soup or protein as a main dish and multiple types of *bancham*, always including some kind of kimchi. The meals are colourful, flavoursome and rich in nutrition.

Egyptian food, like most Middle Eastern food, is robust, rich and quite distinctive, with its own unique ingredients, flavours and textures. Some of the key ingredients are coriander (both fresh and as a spice), cumin and tomatoes. Egyptians tend to use ghee more often than olive oil in cooking, and use olive oil in dressings and dips.

Clay cooking vessels, such as tagines, are popular in Egyptian cooking, just as they are in Moroccan cooking. Shallow clay cooking vessels without lids are used to cook things like *ful*, a dish made from broad beans with cracked eggs over the top. Unlike the northern provinces of the Middle East, such as the Levantine regions, the use of yoghurt in cooking is unheard of – instead, yoghurt is eaten as a side dish, with bread. Egyptian cooking also uses fresh tomatoes and tomato paste a lot – as the base for sauces and in stews.

This book is an homage to the foods that my parents have inspired me to learn how to cook. It is also a reflection of some of the foods that I have learnt about while living in Australia, and have made my own. I hope you will relish the recipes for the textures and flavours they create for you and your loved ones to appreciate!

USE OF SYMBOLS

The recipe is Egyptian in origin

The recipe is Korean in origin

THE FOUR OF US.

HERE I AM WITH MY MUM'S PARENTS, TAEBOK YOU AND BONGSON KANG, AT MY ONE-HUNDRED-DAY CELEBRATION.

MY DAD'S MOTHER, AMINA EL BOGHDADI, AFTER WHOM I WAS NAMED.

WITH MY LITTLE SISTER, EMAN.

Middle Eastern pantry

❀❀❀

BAHARAT
A popular spice blend used in Middle Eastern cookery. The basic version usually has cinnamon, cloves, black pepper and cardamom, but there are many variations. Its robust flavour works particularly well with meats, stews and rich sauces.

BARBERRIES
Barberries (*zereshk* in Persian) are dried red berries commonly used in Persian and North African cooking, usually with meats or couscous. They add a bright pop of colour and a strong, tart flavour. Look for them at Middle Eastern grocery stores, or specialty or gourmet food stores.

BREAD
Several varieties of bread can be found throughout the Middle East. In Egyptian cuisine the most popular is a type of flatbread known as *eish baladi* (country's bread). It is about the size of a hand with a light golden colour and soft, pillow-like texture to help absorb rich sauces. The closest match in Australia would be Turkish bread, so use this or even Lebanese bread whenever my recipes call for bread.

CHINESE/KOREAN CHIVES
Also known as 'garlic chives', these grass-like herbs can be found in Korean and Chinese grocery stores. They have an intensely pungent aroma and are used to make *kimchi* or eaten with grilled meats.

MASTIC
Mastic is a type of resin derived from the mastic tree and is traditionally produced on the Greek island of Chios. The resin comes in small, hard, droplet-like formations that have a light yellow tone and add a distinct, musk-like flavour and aroma. Mastic can be found at Middle Eastern and Greek grocery stores, as well as specialty spice stores.

OLIVE OIL
For most Arabs, olive oil is an essential ingredient. In my household, extra virgin olive oil (first press of olives) is used for dipping bread into, as a garnish or in salad dressings. This way the rich, fresh flavour of the oil may be appreciated. We don't really use virgin olive oil (second press of olives), but often cook with third-press oil, known simply as olive oil, which has a mild flavour that won't overpower other ingredients. Supermarkets stock several international varieties, but Australian olive oils are very flavoursome and well regarded internationally, so I suggest you give them a go.

PARSLEY

Middle Eastern cooks always use flat-leaf parsley rather than the curly variety (also known as continental parsley) for flavour. It is readily available at supermarkets and grocery stores throughout Australia.

POMEGRANATE MOLASSES

Pomegranate molasses is a key ingredient in many Middle Eastern cuisines. It is simply pomegranate juice that has been reduced very slowly over low heat until thick and ruby-coloured. It has an incredibly tart flavour and a lovely sweet finish. Look for varieties that are 100 per cent pomegranate, with no added sugar. All Middle Eastern grocery stores sell pomegranate molasses, and these days you can also find it at larger supermarkets and specialty food stores.

SPICES

Spices are widely used throughout the Middle East. The most common ones are cumin, coriander seeds, paprika, cinnamon, cardamom, cloves and black pepper. Different regions also like to use their own specialty spices, for instance, sumac is associated with northern regions of the Middle East, and mastic is used in countries such as Turkey, Syria and Lebanon. I caution against bulk-buying as spices start to lose their aroma and potency after a couple of months. Instead, buy what you need in small quantities, store them in airtight containers, and replenish as required.

TAGINE

A tagine is a conical-shaped cooking vessel used widely in Northern Africa, however it is best known as a signature of Moroccan cooking. This amazing vessel cooks in a unique way: it collects the steam within the conical lid and allows the resulting condensation to return to the food being cooked inside, resulting in very flavoursome, tender meat and vegetables. Tagines with a decorative glazed coating have lead in the glaze so it is not advisable to use these for cooking or serving food. They are purely ornamental. You can buy glazed ones especially for cooking from cooking stores. It is important that you season the tagine according to the manufacturer's instructions to prevent cracks or breakage. Always start heating the tagine over low heat, then increase gradually to the desired heat. Tagines work best when cooking slowly over gentle heat, on coals or in the oven over a few hours.

TAHINI

In its most familiar form, tahini is a creamy-coloured thick paste made by crushing white sesame seeds. Black tahini paste is made from black sesame seeds and is far less common. Tahini is used widely in Middle Eastern cooking, either as an ingredient or served on its own. There is a thin layer of oil that sits on the thick paste in every jar, and this should be mixed in well before using the paste – don't discard it. Tahini paste can be found at most Middle Eastern and Greek grocery stores and health-food stores.

Korean pantry

BLACK FUNGUS OR WOOD-EAR MUSHROOM
The names are very different, but they both refer to the same type of mushroom. It is difficult to source this variety fresh, but the dried version is readily available at Korean and Asian grocery stores. You need to rehydrate them before use: to do this, soak them in plenty of room-temperature water for 15–30 minutes, then drain well.

CHINESE CABBAGE
Commonly known as wombok (*baechu* in Korean), this vegetable has a white base and its tips and outer leaves are a vibrant green. Used predominantly in Asian cuisine, wombok is perhaps best known as the key ingredient in traditional kimchi. You will find it at Asian supermarkets and larger fruit and vegetable markets or grocery stores.

DANG MYUN
Made from sweet potato starch, dang myun (or 'cellophane noodles') are a type of noodle used for making *chapchae*, a popular noodle dish, and also a traditional beef soup. These versatile noodles have a slightly chewy texture and absorb the flavours of sauces well. Dang myun can be found at Korean food stores and some larger Chinese supermarkets.

DRIED CHILLIES
Dried chillies are very popular in Korean cooking, and may be used whole or in a powdered or flaked form. Korean food stores generally carry an extensive variety of dried chillies. When cooking Korean recipes I recommend you only use Korean chillies, as other varieties of dried chilli, such as paprika or cayenne pepper, will alter the flavour and texture of the dish.

DRIED SPLIT MUNG BEANS
These days, split mung beans can be found at most supermarkets, not just Korean or Indian food stores. Look for the small yellow-coloured beans that have already had their skins removed.

DWANGJANG PASTE
Dwangjang is a Korean paste made from fermented soy beans. It has a pungent aroma and is traditionally stored in large clay vessels that allow the fermentation process to continue. Dwangjang is a base for many stews, including *dwangjang chigae* and a dipping sauce called *ssamjang*, which is eaten with vegetables.

GARAETTEOK
The Korean rice cake, or *tteok*, comes in many forms. It may be plain, stuffed with savoury fillings (mostly bean pastes), or even sweetened with nuts, cinnamon or dried fruits. Garaetteok are white rice cakes that are formed into long

thin cylinders, and may be found fresh, refrigerated and frozen at Korean food stores. Fresh garaetteok are long, but the refrigerated or frozen varieties are cut into shorter lengths.

GOCHUJANG

Gochujang is one of the most commonly used ingredients in Korean cooking. This thick red paste made with red chillies and fermented soy beans is certainly pungent, but not exceedingly hot in flavour, and is mainly used as a base for sauces and soups or as a dipping sauce. There are many manufacturers of gochujang and Korean food stores will offer a wide range.

KIMCHI

In Korean cuisine, 'kimchi' refers to the process of fermenting vegetables, and the type of vegetable being fermented precedes the word 'kimchi'. The best known version is made with Chinese cabbage (baechu), which is called baechu kimchi in Korean. In every Korean kitchen it is a must to have at least one type of kimchi in the pantry – it is eaten on its own and used in cooking, and is considered to have healthy anti-ageing properties. Look for it at Korean food stores and some Asian grocery stores.

KOCHUKARU

Kochukaru is a dried red chilli powder that comes in several forms, from a fine powder to a coarser flake. Each type is suited to particular dishes, so talk to your Korean grocer about which is the right one for the dish you are planning to cook.

KOREAN SOY SAUCE

Like other Asian countries, Koreans have developed their own varieties of soy sauce, which tend to be less salty than other Asian brands. Korean soy sauces can only be bought from Korean food stores, but if you are unable to find them, Japanese soy sauces probably come closest in flavour and texture.

MYULCHI AEKJOT

Koreans have their own version of fish sauce, known as myulchi aekjot, which is derived from fermented anchovies. This dark, potent sauce is commonly used in kimchi to help with flavour development. Myulchi aekjot can only be found at Korean food stores – if you are unable to track it down, Thai fish sauce will suffice.

NAENG MYUN NOODLES

Made from buckwheat, naeng myun noodles are unique to Korean cooking. They are mostly used in *mool naeng myun*, a cold dish in which noodles, cucumbers, nashi pear and thinly sliced cooked beef are served in a chilled broth. They are also used in cold noodle salads with a spicy chilli sauce and mixed vegetables.

SESAME OIL

Sesame oil is an essential item in every Korean kitchen, and is available from all Asian supermarkets and grocery stores, Korean or otherwise. Just make sure you read the label to ensure you are buying 100 per cent sesame oil, as some manufacturers blend in other oils. Pure sesame oil is incredibly rich and flavoursome.

TOASTED SEAWEED

Seaweed has various uses in Korean cooking, including *kimpap* (the Korean version of sushi rolls), as a side dish with rice or as a garnish. Packaged toasted seaweed, which is toasted with sesame oil and salt, is sold at Korean grocery stores.

STARTERS

-1-

STARTERS

There are a number of features that help create a great starter – interesting texture, an incredible pop of flavour, an enticing colour, easy-to-eat portions and real freshness. In my opinion, starters have two purposes. First, to encourage people to share food, mingle and chat. Second, starters should thrill the palate and prepare it for the main meal yet to come.

Starters are not a big feature in Korean cuisine, but I have noticed that Korean restaurants in western countries sometimes serve dishes that are generally eaten as *bancham* (side dishes) as starters, or even offer small portions of main courses.

In Middle Eastern cuisine, starters are often called *mezze*. These are served on small plates and are abundant in variety, and they're often compared to Spanish tapas. The word *mezze* is believed to have come from the Persian language, meaning 'to taste or savour'. Contrary to popular belief, *mezze* are not limited to starters, but can also be eaten as part of the main meal. When the selection is generous and wholesome, it may entertain the diner so well gastronomically that there is no more room for any mains!

This chapter of starters includes recipes that are both nutritious and full of flavour – they will tantalise your loved ones and leave them asking for more!

Baba ghanoush

MUTTABAL

This is my family's favourite dip. It is important to cook the eggplant over an open flame to ensure you get the smoky flavour achieved by charring the skin – otherwise the eggplant flesh will be flavourless. This dip is especially delicious with roast or barbecued lamb. If you are having a barbecue, cook the eggplants before the meat; that way, you can complete the dip by the time the meat is cooked. Always use large eggplants; they have a lot more flesh and are much easier to skin than small ones.

=== MAKES ABOUT 2 CUPS (560 G) ===

3 large eggplants (aubergines)
¼ cup (60 ml) olive oil
½ cup (140 g) tahini
½ cup (125 ml) lemon juice

2 tablespoons finely chopped
  flat-leaf parsley
salt and freshly ground black pepper
extra virgin olive oil, to drizzle
flatbread, to serve

1 Preheat the oven to 180°C.

2 Use a sharp knife to cut deep slits into the eggplants. Using tongs, place the eggplants over an open flame, turning every few minutes until the skin blackens and blisters – about 6–8 minutes.

3 Place the charred eggplants on a baking tray. Cook in the oven for 20 minutes or until the flesh is soft. If you are using a barbecue, place the eggplants over medium heat, turning every few minutes until they are cooked through and soft.

4 Cover the eggplants tightly with plastic film and leave to cool to room temperature. As soon as the eggplants are cool, carefully peel away the skins.

5 Place the peeled eggplant, olive oil, tahini and lemon juice in a food processor and blend until smooth. Mix in the parsley and season with salt and pepper to taste. Spoon into a bowl and drizzle with a little extra virgin olive oil. Serve with flatbread.

6 This dip can be kept in an airtight container in the fridge for up to 3 days.

Beetroot and yoghurt salad

SHAMANDR BI ZABADY

I first tasted this salad on a visit to my father's home in Alexandria, Egypt, when I was thirteen. My grandmother, also known as Tayta, dressed the beetroot simply with garlic, lemon juice and olive oil and I fell in love with the combination of sweetness and tang, and its vibrant, robust colour. I recently decided to recreate this simple, yet wonderful dish, and it is now an absolute favourite among my family and friends.

=== SERVES 4 ===

600 g beetroot (4 medium-sized beetroot), trimmed and peeled

¼ cup (70 g) Greek-style yoghurt

1 tablespoon olive oil

½ teaspoon salt

1 clove garlic, finely chopped

1 tablespoon lemon juice

small handful of mint leaves

extra virgin olive oil, to garnish

1 Place the beetroot in a saucepan of cold water. Bring to the boil, then reduce the heat to a simmer and cook the beetroot for 45 minutes or until you can easily pass a skewer through the centre.

2 Remove the beetroot from the pan and rinse under cold water, then allow to cool to room temperature. Cut the beetroot into thin wedges and arrange on a serving platter.

3 Combine the yoghurt, olive oil, salt, garlic and lemon juice in a small bowl.

4 Drizzle the yoghurt dressing over the beetroot. Garnish with the mint leaves and extra virgin olive oil.

CLOCKWISE FROM LEFT:

CHICKPEA AND TAHINI DIP P 24
CUCUMBER, MINT AND YOGHURT DIP P 25
BEETROOT AND YOGHURT SALAD P 22

Chickpea
and tahini dip

HUMMUS BI TAHINA

Hummus is a classic Middle Eastern starter or *mezze* dish. It is a perfect accompaniment to grilled meats and also tastes good on its own with fresh flatbread. If you can, use the small dried chickpeas rather than the large ones, as this will shorten the soaking and cooking times. You'll need to start this recipe the day before. *Pictured page 23.*

=========== **MAKES ABOUT 2 CUPS (560 G)** ===========

1½ cups (300 g) dried chickpeas
1 teaspoon bicarbonate of soda
½ cup (125 ml) lemon juice, or to taste
¾ cup (210 g) tahini
2 cloves garlic, peeled

salt and freshly ground black pepper
extra virgin olive oil and sweet paprika,
  to garnish
flatbread, to serve

1 Place the chickpeas in a large bowl of water and soak for 12 hours, changing the water around halfway through soaking. Rinse and drain the chickpeas.

2 Place the chickpeas in a saucepan of cold water. Bring to the boil, then reduce the heat to a simmer. Add the bicarbonate of soda and cook for about 2 hours or until the chickpeas are very soft and can be easily squashed between two fingers. Drain, reserving 1 cup (250 ml) of the cooking liquid, then remove any loose skins and leave the chickpeas to cool to room temperature or refrigerate them overnight.

3 Place the cooled chickpeas in a food processor with the lemon juice, tahini and garlic and blend until well combined. If the mixture is very thick, add some of the reserved cooking liquid, a tablespoon at a time, to achieve a smoother consistency. Alternatively, you can add more lemon juice, according to taste.

4 Season to taste with salt and pepper, then transfer to a shallow bowl and finish with a generous drizzle of olive oil and a sprinkle of sweet paprika. Serve with flatbread.

5 This dip can be kept in an airtight container in the fridge for up to 5 days.

Cucumber, mint and yoghurt dip

ZABADY BI KHIYAR WA NA'NAA

This dip is very similar to the famous tzatziki, however it is made in a slightly different way. Yoghurt is a staple ingredient in Middle Eastern cooking, especially in the northern regions such as Lebanon, Syria and Turkey. My family enjoys this dip with roast lamb or served as a *mezze* with fresh bread. *Pictured page 23.*

=== MAKES ABOUT 2 CUPS (560 G) ===

1 Lebanese (short) cucumber
1 cup (280 g) Greek-style yoghurt
1 tablespoon finely chopped mint
1 small clove garlic, minced

1 tablespoon extra virgin olive oil,
  plus extra to garnish
1 tablespoon lemon juice
salt

1 Finely grate the cucumber, then place in a sieve and press down gently to remove as much liquid as possible.

2 Place the strained cucumber, yoghurt, mint, garlic, tablespoon of olive oil and lemon juice in a bowl and mix well. Taste and season with salt, if required. Transfer to a shallow bowl and garnish with a little extra virgin olive oil. Serve.

3 This dip can be kept in an airtight container in the fridge for up to 2 days.

Tayta's salad

This is another of my Egyptian grandmother's recipes. I have fond memories of her ability to create salads by chopping up vegetables without using a chopping board! She would chop the salad ingredients into small, bite-sized pieces and finish with a simple lemon and olive oil dressing. This is a recipe based on my family's favourite salad ingredients, which can be easily found all year round.

=== SERVES 4 ===

1 Lebanese (short) cucumber
1 carrot
4 tomatoes
2 small radishes
¼ red onion
1 spring onion, trimmed and thinly sliced
large handful of rocket, roughly chopped
small handful of flat-leaf parsley leaves,
    roughly chopped

DRESSING
¼ cup (60 ml) lemon juice
2 tablespoons extra virgin olive oil
½ teaspoon ground cumin
salt

1 To make the dressing, place the lemon juice, olive oil and cumin in a small bowl and mix well. Season with salt to taste.

2 Chop the cucumber, carrot, tomatoes, radishes and red onion into small cubes all roughly the same size, and place them in a large bowl.

3 Add the spring onion, rocket and parsley to the bowl.

4 Either toss with the dressing, or serve dressing on the side, and serve immediately.

CLOCKWISE FROM LEFT:

TAYTA'S SALAD P 26
FATTOUSH P 28

Fattoush

I made fattoush as one of my audition dishes to get into the Top 24 of *MasterChef*. This iconic Middle Eastern salad incorporates crunchy bread, fresh vegetables and a unique purple dressing that has an incredible sweet-and-sour flavour. If you have never tried it before, I encourage you to make fattoush this summer for yourself and your family. *Pictured page 27.*

===== SERVES 4 =====

1 flatbread
1 Lebanese (short) cucumber,
    cut into 1 cm cubes
3 firm tomatoes, cut into 1 cm cubes
handful of flat-leaf parsley leaves,
    roughly chopped
small handful of mint leaves,
    roughly chopped
2 radishes, cut into 1 cm cubes
1 spring onion, trimmed and thinly sliced
1 small red capsicum (pepper), seeds and
    membrane discarded, cut into 1 cm cubes
4 iceberg lettuce leaves, finely shredded

DRESSING
¼ cup (60 ml) extra virgin olive oil
¼ cup (60 ml) lemon juice
2 tablespoons pomegranate molasses
1 teaspoon sumac
¾ teaspoon salt
pinch of freshly ground black pepper

1 Preheat the oven to 180°C.

2 To make the dressing, place all the ingredients in a small bowl and mix well.

3 Toast the flatbread in the oven for about 4 minutes, until crisp and golden.

4 Place all the remaining salad ingredients in a large bowl, add the dressing and toss lightly. Crumble the bread over the top and serve immediately.

Eggplant with cumin vinaigrette

One family holiday to Egypt, while wandering the streets of Alexandria looking for a snack we came across a great sandwich shop that served this delicious eggplant dish in a sandwich with potato chips – a far more enticing option than the cow's brain sandwich also on offer!

===== SERVES 4–6 =====

2 large eggplants (aubergines), stems
    removed, cut into 1 cm thick slices
salt
1 litre vegetable oil, for deep-frying
coriander leaves, to garnish
½ teaspoon chilli flakes
flatbread, to serve

CUMIN VINAIGRETTE
¾ cup (180 ml) white vinegar
1 large clove garlic, minced
1 teaspoon ground cumin
½ teaspoon salt

1 Sprinkle the eggplant slices generously with salt and place in a bowl for 30 minutes to remove any bitterness.

2 To make the cumin vinaigrette, place all the ingredients in a small bowl and mix well.

3 Rinse the eggplant slices well under cold running water and place in a colander for 15 minutes to drain. Pat them dry with paper towels if there is excess water.

4 Heat the vegetable oil in a deep saucepan until it registers 180°C on a thermometer (or a cube of bread dropped into the oil browns in 20 seconds). Deep-fry the eggplant, in batches, for 2–4 minutes, until the flesh is slightly golden. Remove and drain on paper towels.

5 Place a layer of fried eggplant in a shallow bowl and spoon half of the cumin vinaigrette over the top. Layer the remaining eggplant on top, then dress with the remaining vinaigrette. Garnish with coriander and chilli flakes, and serve with flatbread.

Pomegranate and walnut salad

SALATAH BI ROMMAAN WA JOOZ

This crunchy, tangy and vibrant salad is closely related to the classic Turkish 'spoon salad'. Everything is cut into very small pieces so that one spoonful of the salad excites the palate with all the different ingredients. I have been making it at home a lot over the last couple of years, especially as part of a weekend lunch spread. It is a great accompaniment to quail or red meat.

=== SERVES 4 ===

½ cup (50 g) walnuts
1 pomegranate, cut in half
large handful of flat-leaf parsley leaves, roughly chopped
2 tomatoes, cut into very small cubes
1 Lebanese (short) cucumber, seeded and cut into very small cubes
½ red capsicum (pepper), seeds and membrane discarded, cut into very small cubes

½ red onion, finely chopped
1 teaspoon sumac
2 tablespoons extra virgin olive oil
2 tablespoons lemon juice
1 tablespoon pomegranate molasses
salt

1 Preheat the oven to 200°C. Place the walnuts on a baking tray and toast in the oven for 5–7 minutes. Remove from the oven and allow to cool, then roughly chop.

2 Hold a pomegranate half over a large bowl and, using a wooden spoon, tap the pomegranate hard to release the arils (seeds). Repeat with the other half.

3 Add the walnuts, parsley, tomato, cucumber, capsicum, onion and sumac to the bowl.

4 Stir in the olive oil, lemon juice and pomegranate molasses and toss to combine. Season with salt to taste and serve immediately.

String haloumi and sumac salad

SALATAH HALOUMI WAS SUMMAK

In Australia, there are many dairy manufacturers now making traditional Middle Eastern dairy products. String haloumi is a perfect example. This lightly salted cheese is eaten fresh, not cooked, and is known as string cheese because the cheese is formed into long thin strands. In this recipe, the haloumi soaks up the tart dressing beautifully and looks spectacular on the plate. String haloumi is available from Middle Eastern grocery stores, but if you can't find any, use reduced-fat haloumi sliced into long, thin strips instead. This salad is also great served as part of a selection of *mezze*.

=== SERVES 4 ===

2 tablespoons extra virgin olive oil
2 tablespoons lemon juice
1 teaspoon sumac, plus a little extra,
    to garnish
150 g string haloumi, pulled apart
3 small radishes, thinly sliced

8 cherry tomatoes, quartered
small handful of flat-leaf parsley leaves,
    roughly chopped
small handful of mint leaves,
    roughly chopped
2 tablespoons pomegranate seeds

1 Combine the olive oil, lemon juice and sumac in a large bowl. Add the separated strands of haloumi, radish, tomato and herbs.

2 Toss lightly together to coat all the ingredients with the dressing.

3 Scatter the pomegranate seeds over the top, sprinkle with extra sumac and serve.

Kimchi pancakes

KIMCHI BINDADOK

My mother would tell me stories about how my grandfather (*Haraboji*) always made these pancakes for the family on rainy days, so for her this is a particularly sentimental dish. There are many different varieties of kimchi (which means 'fermented' in Korean), but in western countries the word usually refers to the traditional Chinese cabbage (wombok) variety. Here, you could use some of the Baechu kimchi in the recipe on page 71 or you could buy some kimchi from a Korean food store. Start this recipe the day before.

MAKES 12 PANCAKES

440 g dried split mung beans
  (see page 11), rinsed
⅓ cup (65 g) short-grain rice, rinsed
⅓ cup (80 ml) kimchi liquid
⅓ cup (80 ml) water
2 cups (160 g) bean sprouts
140 g kimchi, squeezed (liquid reserved;
  see above) and finely chopped
  (see page 12)
1 small bunch Chinese/Korean chives
  (see page 7), cut into 2 cm lengths
3 spring onions, trimmed and thinly sliced
  on the diagonal

1 long green chilli, thinly sliced
  on the diagonal
1 long red chilli, thinly sliced
  on the diagonal
1 tablespoon soy sauce
1 tablespoon sesame oil
salt and freshly ground black pepper
vegetable oil, for frying

DIPPING SAUCE
¼ cup (60 ml) dark soy sauce
2 tablespoons white vinegar

1 Place the mung beans and rice in a large bowl and cover with water. Place the bowl in the fridge for at least 8 hours or overnight. Rinse the beans and rice, and drain well.

2 To make the dipping sauce, combine the soy sauce and vinegar in a small bowl.

3 In a food processor, blitz the mung beans and rice with the kimchi liquid and water until the mixture forms a smooth paste. Transfer to a large bowl and set aside.

4 Bring a saucepan of water to the boil and blanch the bean sprouts for 2 minutes, then drain and rinse them under cold water. Using a muslin cloth or just your hands, squeeze as much liquid as possible from the bean sprouts, then cut them into 2 cm lengths.

5 Add the bean sprouts, chopped kimchi, chives, spring onion, green and red chilli, soy sauce, sesame oil and salt and pepper to the mung bean and rice paste and mix well.

6 Heat a well-oiled, heavy-based frying pan over medium heat. Once hot, use a small ladle to pour in enough batter to form a pancake 15 cm in diameter. Cook for at least 3–4 minutes on each side, so that the inside is cooked through and the outside is slightly crisp. Repeat the process to make about 12 pancakes, ensuring that the pan is oiled for each one.

7 Serve the kimchi pancakes warm with the dipping sauce.

Pan-fried tofu with chilli and spring onion dressing

TUBU BUCHIM

With its health benefits, unique texture and ability to absorb other flavours, tofu is very popular in western food culture. In Korea, tofu or *tubu* is incorporated into many dishes, particularly stews. My mother has always told us about the benefits of tofu and never goes more than three days without cooking it at home. *Yang nyum jang* is common in Korean cooking as a sauce for fried foods such as tofu; it is also used to add flavour to clear soups.

=== SERVES 4 ===

vegetable oil, for shallow-frying
1 × 400 g packet firm tofu
    (preferably Korean),
    sliced into 2 cm pieces

YANG NYUM JANG DRESSING
1 tablespoon sesame seeds
⅓ cup (80 ml) Korean soy sauce
    (see page 12)
2 spring onions, trimmed and thinly sliced
2 cloves garlic, crushed
2 tablespoons kochukaru (Korean chilli
    powder; see page 12)
2 tablespoons sesame oil

1 To make the dressing, toast the sesame seeds in a dry frying pan over medium heat for about 3 minutes, until golden and fragrant. Combine all the remaining ingredients in a small bowl, add the toasted sesame seeds and mix well. Set aside.

2 Heat vegetable oil in a non-stick frying pan over medium heat. Fry the tofu in two batches, cooking for 2–3 minutes on each side, until it is golden and slightly crisp. Add a little more oil to the pan before cooking the second batch.

3 Arrange the tofu on a serving platter and spoon a small amount of sauce over the top. You won't need very much as the sauce is quite strong. Serve immediately.

4 Store the remaining sauce in an airtight container in the fridge for up to 1 month.

Vegetable bites

YACHA TIGIM

There are some similarities between Korean and Japanese cuisine, and these vegetable bites are a good example as they're similar to Japanese tempura. This recipe uses sweet potato, onion and zucchini, but feel free to experiment with other vegetables as well.

——— SERVES 6 ———

1 sweet potato, peeled
  and very finely sliced
1 onion, finely sliced
1 zucchini (courgette), very finely sliced
1 red chilli, seeded and finely sliced
vegetable oil, for shallow-frying

DIPPING SAUCE
2 tablespoons soy sauce
2 tablespoons white vinegar
1 teaspoon white sugar
pinch of kochukaru (Korean chilli
  powder; see page 12)

BATTER
1 cup (150 g) plain flour
½ cup (75 g) cornflour
1 teaspoon salt
½ teaspoon freshly ground black pepper
1 egg, lightly beaten
1 cup (250 ml) cold water

1 To make the dipping sauce, place all the ingredients in a small bowl and mix well until the sugar dissolves. Set aside.

2 To make the batter, place the flour, cornflour, salt and pepper in a deep bowl. Slowly add the egg and cold water and whisk well to form a thick batter, making sure there are no lumps.

3 Add the vegetables, one type at a time, and mix gently until they are lightly covered in the batter.

4 Heat about 3 cm of vegetable oil in a large, shallow pan until it registers 180°C on a thermometer (or a cube of bread dropped into the oil browns in 20 seconds).

5 Remove the vegetables from the batter one at a time, gently shaking to remove any excess, then carefully drop them into the hot oil. You will need to fry them in batches to avoid overcrowding the pan. Cook for 3–4 minutes, until golden and crispy, turning to ensure even cooking. Remove from the pan using chopsticks or a slotted spoon and drain on paper towels.

6 Eat straight away with the dipping sauce.

Clay-steamed egg

TUKBAEGI GAERANJIM

This light and delicate dish makes a lovely starter. My Korean grandmother (my *halmony*) showed me this method of steaming the egg in a traditional clay bowl within a saucepan of boiling water. She taught me how to grease the inside of the bowl lightly so that the egg does not stick. Korean stores sell these black or dark-grey clay vessels, but you could always use a large, heavy ramekin as an alternative.

=== SERVES 2 ===

4 eggs
½ cup (125 ml) water
1 spring onion, trimmed and thinly sliced
1 teaspoon fish sauce

½ teaspoon salt
pinch of freshly ground black pepper
vegetable oil, for greasing

1 Crack the eggs into a mixing bowl. Add the water and whisk until well combined and bubbly. Add the spring onion, fish sauce, salt and pepper.

2 Lightly grease a medium clay bowl with vegetable oil and pour in the egg mixture.

3 Choose a saucepan larger than the clay bowl and fill it with 5 cm of water. Bring to the boil over medium heat, then carefully place the clay bowl inside. Place a lid on the saucepan and steam for 10 minutes. Check the mixture is cooked by inserting a skewer; if it is not, leave for a further 2 minutes. Carefully remove the clay bowl from the pan.

4 Serve hot.

Steamed kimchi dumplings

KIMCHI MANDU

This is one of our family favourites. During Korean New Year, my mother and aunties used to get together and make hundreds of dumplings to feed the whole extended family. Although they are a bit fiddly, the end result is sensational. You could use some of the Baechu kimchi on page 71 in the filling, or buy some kimchi from a Korean food store. You can also make a vegetarian version by replacing the meat with more tofu.

=== SERVES 4 ===

20–30 white round wonton wrappers
   (or eggless wonton wrappers)
Dipping Sauce (see Vegetable Bites,
   page 39), to serve

FILLING
100 g beef mince
100 g firm tofu, crumbled
1 spring onion, trimmed and finely chopped
1 egg
2 tablespoons kimchi, squeezed
   and finely chopped (see page 71)
2 tablespoons finely chopped Chinese/
   Korean chives (see page 7)
2 tablespoons sesame oil
1 tablespoon Korean soy sauce
   (see page 12)
½ teaspoon salt
pinch of freshly ground black pepper

1 Place all the filling ingredients in a large bowl. Mix with your hands until well combined and free of chunks.

2 Place 1 teaspoon of the filling in the centre of a wonton wrapper. Lightly dab water around the edge of the wrapper, then fold into a half-moon to enclose the filling. Crimp the edges with your fingers to ensure the dumpling is sealed. Repeat with the remaining filling and wonton wrappers.

3 Line a bamboo steamer with baking paper. Add the dumplings a few at a time and steam over boiling water for 5–8 minutes, until cooked through.

4 Serve immediately with dipping sauce.

Sweet potato with honey

GOGUMA MAT-TANG

These sticky sweet potatoes can be found everywhere on the streets of South Korea. They are usually sold on skewers to show off their delicious golden sheen, and they are very hard to resist! I especially love eating them with hot, fluffy white rice.

=== SERVES 4 ===

2 large sweet potatoes, peeled
   and cut into bite-sized cubes
3 cups (750 ml) vegetable oil
¾ cup (180 ml) water

½ cup (180 g) honey
1 tablespoon black sesame seeds
½ teaspoon salt

1 Soak the sweet potato in a bowl of salted water for 20 minutes. Drain and dry well with paper towels.

2 Heat the vegetable oil in a large heavy-based saucepan until it registers 180°C on a thermometer (or a cube of bread dropped into the oil browns in 20 seconds). Deep-fry the sweet potato in batches, turning regularly, for about 4–5 minutes, until they are golden-brown. Remove and drain on paper towels.

3 In a large wok, heat the water over medium heat, then add the honey and mix well for about 3 minutes, until thickened. Quickly add the sweet potato, sesame seeds and salt, then reduce the heat to low and cook for a few minutes, until the sweet potato is glossy and the sauce is thick and sticky. Serve warm.

Skewered beef and vegetables

PASANJEOK

This dish is revered by most Korean families. Koreans have many traditions, one of which is that on the anniversary of a family member's death, the family pays its respects by gathering together, preparing the favourite foods of the deceased and then presenting them beautifully on a table with the deceased's picture above. The family members then perform a ritual, with each one bowing to the deceased as a mark of respect. Afterwards, the family sits together and celebrates the memory of their loved one with the foods made for the ceremony. My mother's family, the Kangs, always makes this dish on the anniversary of my grandfather's death, and everyone enjoys it in his memory.

MAKES 10

250 g beef sirloin steak, tenderised and
    cut into 20 strips, each 5 cm long
1 large carrot, cut into 20 batons,
    each 5 cm long
10 spring onions, trimmed, white and green
    parts separated, then each cut into
    5 cm batons
¼ cup (60 ml) vegetable oil

MARINADE
1 tablespoon sesame oil
1 tablespoon soy sauce
1 teaspoon white sugar
1 clove garlic, minced
pinch of freshly ground black pepper

BATTER
1 cup (150 g) plain flour
1 cup (250 ml) water
½ teaspoon salt

1 To make the marinade, place all the ingredients in a large bowl and mix well.

2 Add the beef strips to the marinade and mix gently to coat. Place in the fridge for 1 hour to marinate.

3 Bring a saucepan of salted water to the boil and blanch the carrot and white spring onion batons for about 1 minute. Cool immediately in a bowl of cold water, then drain.

4 Place one carrot baton, one meat strip and one white spring onion baton on top of each other, then place one carrot baton, one green spring onion baton and one meat strip on top of this, so you have a stack of six elements. Using two toothpicks, skewer the stack at each end to secure it. Repeat until you have made 10 stacks.

5 Place the batter ingredients in a bowl and whisk well until there are no lumps.

6 Heat the vegetable oil in a non-stick frying pan over medium heat. Dip the stacks into the batter, draining off any excess. Working in batches, carefully place the stacks in the frying pan and fry for about 3 minutes on each side, until the meat is just cooked. Serve warm.

CLOCKWISE FROM TOP:

HERB AND LEMON MARINATED OLIVES P 51
DUKKAH SERVED WITH LABNA P 49
MOROCCAN CARROTS WITH HONEY, MINT AND CINNAMON P 50

Dukkah
served with labna

DUKKAH WA LABNA

Dukkah is, of course, wonderful served as a dip accompanied by fresh bread and some good-quality extra virgin olive oil (as well as delicious cheeses), but I have recently discovered many other ways to use this versatile spice and nut mix. One of my favourites is to add a little olive oil to make a paste, then spread a thick layer over lamb or salmon before you cook it to create a delicious crust. I have used hazelnuts here for a gourmet touch, but in Egypt dukkah is traditionally made with peanuts as they are more affordable. Serve it with labna, a deliciously tart strained yoghurt cheese, available from Middle Eastern grocers or delicatessens.

—— MAKES 2 CUPS (ABOUT 300 G) ——

1 cup (150 g) sesame seeds
75 g coriander seeds
75 g cumin seeds
¾ cup (105 g) skinless hazelnuts

salt
¼ cup (70 g) labna
extra virgin olive oil, to garnish
flatbread, to serve

1 Toast the sesame seeds in a dry frying pan over medium heat for about 3 minutes, until golden and fragrant. Transfer to a bowl and cool to room temperature.

2 Toast the coriander seeds and cumin seeds separately in a heavy-based frying pan over medium heat, shaking the pan occasionally, for about 3–4 minutes or until fragrant, but not smoking. Transfer to separate bowls and cool to room temperature.

3 Preheat the oven to 180°C. Spread the hazelnuts over a baking tray and roast for 5 minutes, until golden, shaking the tray once to ensure even roasting, then remove from the oven and cool to room temperature.

4 Using a mortar and pestle or a spice grinder, pound or process the sesame seeds, coriander seeds, cumin seeds and hazelnuts individually until they are quite coarse, but not finely ground.

5 Combine the sesame seeds, coriander seeds, cumin seeds and hazelnuts in a bowl and season to taste with salt.

6 Spoon the labna onto a plate and top with a generous amount of the dukkah. Drizzle with extra virgin olive oil and serve with flatbread.

7 Store the remaining dukkah in an airtight container for up to 2 months or freeze it for up to 4 months.

Moroccan carrots with honey, mint and cinnamon

Heirloom carrots are as stunning as they are delicious. This dish traditionally uses orange carrots, but it becomes even more beautiful if you include the purple and white varieties as well. The honey glaze, cut through by the fresh mint, is a perfect accompaniment. I first tasted this dish when I was in Marrakesh. It accompanied a lovely beef tagine and couscous, and I was so taken by it that I had to ask the waiter how it was made. My father absolutely loves carrots, so this was a winning dish for him, too! *Pictured page 48.*

——— SERVES 4 ———

1 tablespoon olive oil
2 bunches baby (Dutch) heirloom carrots, peeled and trimmed, leaving 5 cm stalk
⅓ cup (80 ml) orange juice, strained
1 teaspoon ground cinnamon

1 tablespoon honey
20 g unsalted butter
½ teaspoon salt
2 tablespoons finely chopped mint

1 Heat the olive oil in a non-stick frying pan over medium heat, add the carrots and cook for 2 minutes, shaking the pan regularly so the carrots don't stick. Stir in the orange juice and cinnamon and reduce the heat to a gentle simmer for 2 minutes. Add the honey and butter, increase the heat to high and cook for about 1 minute more, until the carrots are coated in a sticky glaze.

2 Remove the carrots from the heat, add the salt and mint and toss lightly to combine.

3 Serve warm.

Herb and lemon marinated olives

ZAITOUN BI 'ASHAB

My parents absolutely adore olives. My mother makes a batch every year, around the start of autumn, at the end of harvest time. She buys boxes of black and green olives straight from the growers at the Sydney Markets at Flemington and then undertakes the long process of washing and drying them and making the brine. After the olives have soaked in the brine for a few months, I wash them and make this lovely marinade, which adds even more depth and flavour. These are especially addictive served with cheese.

To sterilise the jar, wash it in hot, soapy water, then rinse before placing in a large saucepan of boiling water. After 10 minutes, remove the jar and drain it on a clean tea towel. Place in an oven set at 150°C and dry. Using tongs, remove the jar from the oven and allow to cool before filling with the olives and marinade. *Pictured page 48.*

================ MAKES 850 G JAR ================

200 g drained large green olives in brine
200 g drained large black olives in brine
1 red chilli, seeded and thinly sliced
1 preserved lemon, rind only, rinsed
   and thinly sliced
½ teaspoon salt flakes

2 sprigs oregano
2 sprigs thyme
2 sprigs marjoram
1 teaspoon sumac
1½ cups (375 ml) olive oil

1 Wash the olives several times under cool running water to remove any brine, then dry them well with a clean tea towel. Using a sharp knife, carefully cut two deep slits into each olive.

2 Combine all the remaining ingredients in a large bowl and add the olives, stirring gently to coat them thoroughly with the marinade. Transfer the contents to a sterilised jar and leave to marinate in the fridge for 3 days, stirring the olives once a day to ensure they are well coated. Use a clean, dry spoon when accessing the jar to avoid the introduction of bacteria that could spoil the olives.

3 The marinated olives will keep for up to 2 months in the fridge.

Savoury lady finger pastries with mint yoghurt sauce

Your family and guests will love these delicious parcels! They are great for entertaining, and taste especially good straight out of the oven. Barberries are used commonly in Persian cooking and can be found at Persian or Afghan grocery stores. If you cannot find barberries, dried cranberries or currants are a great substitute.

=== MAKES 20 ===

¼ cup (40 g) pine nuts
2 tablespoons olive oil
1 onion, finely chopped
1 clove garlic, minced
400 g lamb mince
2 tablespoons dried barberries (see page 7)
1 tablespoon baharat (see page 7)
1 teaspoon ground cinnamon
1 tablespoon pomegranate molasses
1 teaspoon salt
1 tablespoon lemon juice
1 × 375 g packet filo pastry
120 g unsalted butter, melted

MINT YOGHURT SAUCE
½ cup (140 g) Greek-style yoghurt
small handful of mint, leaves picked
1 tablespoon extra virgin olive oil
½ teaspoon salt

1 Preheat the oven to 180°C.

2 To make the mint yoghurt sauce, place all the ingredients in a food processor and blitz until the mint is finely chopped and the yoghurt has turned light-green. Refrigerate.

3 Spread the pine nuts out on a baking tray and toast in the oven for about 5 minutes, until golden-brown, shaking the tray occasionally so they don't burn.

4 Heat the olive oil in a frying pan over high heat, add the onion and garlic and cook until translucent. Increase the heat to high, add the mince and cook for 5 minutes or until browned, using a fork to break up the mince as it cooks.

5 Add the toasted pine nuts, barberries, baharat, cinnamon, molasses, salt and lemon juice to the pan and continue to cook for 5 more minutes, until very little liquid remains. Remove from the heat and leave to cool completely.

6 Take one sheet of filo pastry and cut it into thirds lengthways. (Cover the other filo sheets with a damp tea towel while you work to stop them from drying out.) Brush each piece of pastry generously with melted butter. Place one scant tablespoon of the mince mixture at one short end of the pastry and fold in the edges. Roll the pastry into a cigar shape, ensuring the end is sealed off well with melted butter. Repeat the process until you have made 20 lady fingers in all.

7 Place the lady fingers on a lightly greased tray and cook for 20 minutes, or until they are golden and crispy. Serve warm with the mint yoghurt sauce.

VEGETABLES, LEGUMES AND GRAINS

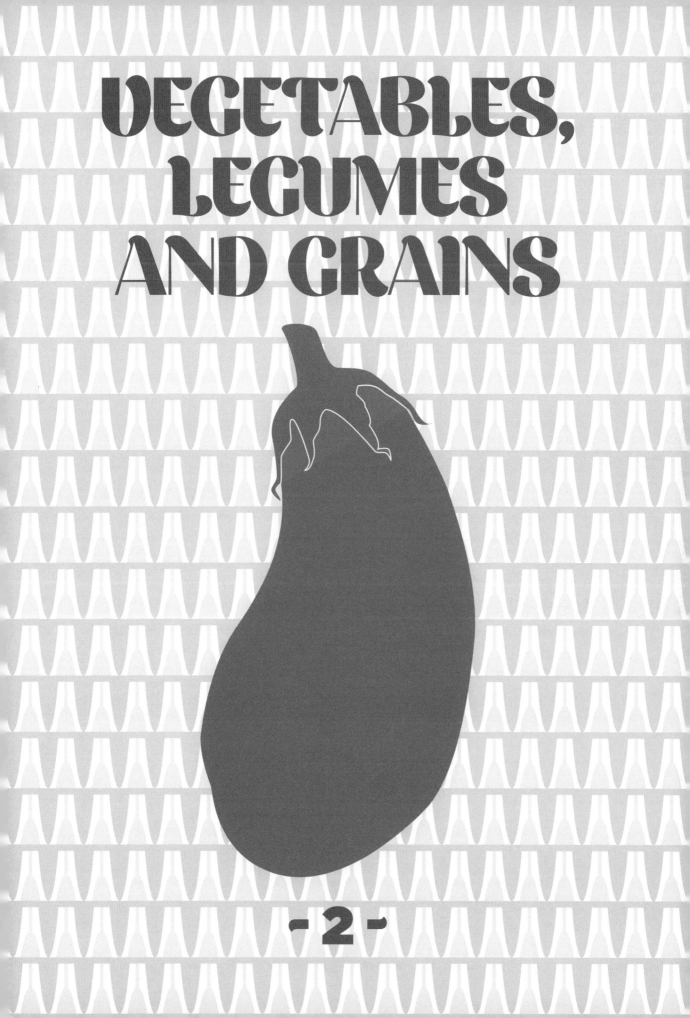

VEGETABLES, LEGUMES AND GRAINS

I am constantly amazed by the incredible variety of vegetables produced in Australia. During my travels around the country I have sampled produce that is a cook's dream to indulge in and experiment with.

My parents have always done their weekly fruit and vegetable shopping at the Sydney Markets in Flemington on a Saturday morning. Eman and I would usually accompany them, and I remember following them closely as they wove their way through the manic crowds.

I now realise that those expeditions taught me invaluable lessons about how to assess the quality of produce and how to bargain! Nowadays, I still enjoy shopping at the markets early on Saturday mornings, as these visits always provide great inspiration.

I also love cooking with legumes – not a big part of Korean cuisine, but very popular in Egyptian cooking, where they are often used in vegetarian dishes. One of my family's favourite dishes is falafel, which in Egypt is made from broad beans. Broad beans are also used in another renowned Egyptian dish called *ful*, a version of baked beans whose history can be traced back to ancient Egyptian civilisation.

Grains, especially rice, are an integral part of both Korean and Egyptian cuisines. Korean cuisine uses a short- to medium-grain rice, sometimes integrating wild rice grains, such as black or brown rice. It is also common to mix rice with small dried red beans or barley, for a healthier approach. In Egyptian cuisine, a medium- to long-grain rice is preferred, often cooked with ghee or butter to loosen the grains and add richness.

Stuffed eggplant and zucchini

MAHSHI BATINGAN WA KOUSA

My mum loves going to the markets with my father and buying a selection of small vegetables, such as eggplants and zucchini, to stuff. She claims she makes this dish because Dad loves it so much, but I think she enjoys it even more herself! The key is to cook it gently so the vegetables retain their shape and the rice becomes soft, while both are delicately flavoured by the spices and herbs.

——— SERVES 4–6 ———

1½ cups (300 g) short-grain rice
8 baby zucchini (courgettes)
8 Japanese eggplants (aubergines),
   stalks trimmed
½ cup (80 g) pine nuts
2 tomatoes
small handful of coriander, leaves picked
small handful of flat-leaf parsley,
   leaves picked
small handful of dill, fronds picked
1 large onion, roughly chopped

4 cloves garlic, crushed
2 teaspoons ground cinnamon
1 tablespoon baharat (see page 7)
1 teaspoon ground cumin
1 teaspoon salt
½ teaspoon freshly ground black pepper
4 cups (1 kg) passata
1 litre vegetable stock
¼ cup (60 ml) olive oil
extra virgin olive oil, to drizzle

1 Soak the rice in salted water for 30 minutes, then rinse and drain.

2 Meanwhile, use an apple corer to carefully hollow out the inside of each zucchini and eggplant, leaving the bases intact. Be very careful not to pierce or break the vegetable skins.

3 Preheat the oven to 180°C. Spread the pine nuts over a baking tray and toast in the oven for about 5 minutes, until golden-brown, shaking the tray occasionally so they don't burn.

4 Halve the tomatoes, then squeeze out the seeds and pulp, and discard. In a food processor, blitz the tomato, coriander, parsley, dill, onion and garlic until well combined. Place the mixture in a bowl and add the soaked rice, toasted pine nuts, cinnamon, baharat, cumin, salt and pepper. Mix well with your hands. Spoon the rice mixture into the zucchini and eggplant shells, being careful not to overfill them.

5 Heat the passata, vegetable stock and olive oil in a saucepan until the mixture comes to the boil, then remove from the heat and season with salt and pepper to taste.

6 Spoon in enough of the tomato mixture to cover the bottom of a heavy-based casserole dish. Line the zucchini and eggplants up tightly next to each other and gently cover with the rest of the tomato mixture. Place a heatproof plate on the top of the vegetables to weigh them down, then cover the dish with the lid.

7 Cook over medium–high heat for 5 minutes, until the sauce comes to the boil, then reduce the heat to medium and cook for 1 hour. Turn the heat off and set aside for about 15 minutes to cool slightly.

8 Serve the stuffed vegetables finished with a spoonful of tomato sauce over the top and drizzled with extra virgin olive oil.

Egyptian broad bean falafel

TAAMIYAH

When Eman and I were growing up, my father used to buy falafel every Sunday and make them into delicious rolls for us all to enjoy. Unlike the northern Middle East version which uses chickpeas, the Egyptian version has always had broad beans as the core ingredient. Sometimes, the Egyptians also add a touch of chilli to deliver a hit of heat and ramp up the flavour. You'll need to start this recipe the day before.

=== SERVES 4–6 ===

240 g dried and peeled broad beans
4 cloves garlic, peeled
small handful of coriander, leaves picked
small handful of flat-leaf parsley,
  leaves picked
1 red onion, peeled and quartered
2 tablespoons ground cumin
1 tablespoon ground coriander
½ teaspoon cayenne pepper
1 tablespoon salt
½ teaspoon freshly ground black pepper
1 teaspoon bicarbonate of soda
sesame seeds, to sprinkle
vegetable oil, for deep-frying
salad and pickles, to serve
flatbread, to serve (optional)

TAHINI SAUCE
100 g hulled tahini
⅔ cup (160 ml) water
1 small clove garlic, minced
½ teaspoon ground cumin
salt and freshly ground black pepper

1 Soak the broad beans in cold water for 12 hours, draining and rinsing them about halfway through, then rinse again and leave to drain for 1 hour to remove as much water as possible.

2 Place the broad beans, garlic, herbs, onion, spices, salt, pepper and bicarbonate of soda in a food processor and blitz to a fine grain-like consistency. Transfer the mixture to a large bowl, cover with plastic film and place in the fridge for 1 hour.

3 Meanwhile, to make the tahini sauce, blend all the ingredients using a blender or stick mixer until they form a smooth sauce. Cover with plastic film and place in the fridge until ready to serve.

4 Using 1 tablespoon of the broad bean mixture at a time, carefully shape into a small patty and then sprinkle the falafel with sesame seeds.

5 Heat the vegetable oil in a deep-fryer or saucepan until it registers 180°C on a thermometer (or a cube of bread dropped into the oil browns in 20 seconds).

6 Working in batches, gently lower the falafel into the hot oil and cook for about 3–4 minutes, turning once, until the outside is golden and crunchy and the inside is moist, yet cooked through. Remove the falafel with a slotted spoon and drain on paper towels.

7 Serve the falafel immediately with tahini sauce, salad and pickles, and flatbread if you like.

Slow-cooked broad beans

FUL MEDAMES

This must be the most loved Egyptian breakfast dish. Some Egyptians believe that a day without it for breakfast is not complete! In many ways, it is the Egyptian equivalent of English baked beans – but fragrant and boasting great flavours. *Ful* is also one of the country's oldest recipes, dating back to the time of the Pharaohs; it was one of the easiest ways to feed the workers and keep them full. My uncles like to remind me that as a child I would copy them and call this dish *asmant* ('cement' in Arabic), which gives you an idea of just how filling it is! You'll need to start this dish the day before.

=== SERVES 4–6 ===

2 cups (240 g) dried broad beans, unpeeled
1.2 litres cold water, plus extra if needed
salt and freshly ground black pepper
small handful of flat-leaf parsley, leaves
    picked and finely chopped
1 red onion, finely chopped
2 tomatoes, finely chopped
lemon wedges, to serve
extra virgin olive oil, to drizzle
ground cumin, to sprinkle
flatbread, to serve

SEASONING
¼ cup (60 ml) olive oil
1 large red onion, finely minced
2 cloves garlic, finely chopped
1½ tablespoons ground cumin
1 teaspoon ground coriander
⅓ cup (80 ml) lemon juice, strained

1 Soak the broad beans in cold water for 24 hours, draining and rinsing them about halfway through.

2 Rinse the soaked beans, then place them in a large saucepan and cover with 1.2 litres of water. Bring to the boil over high heat and boil for 2 minutes, skimming to remove any impurities from the surface. Reduce the heat to a gentle simmer and cook the beans, covered, for 3–4 hours. Give them a good stir every half an hour, checking to ensure there is enough liquid remaining in the pan. If the liquid begins to dry up, stir in ⅓ cup (80 ml) of water as necessary.

3 To prepare the seasoning, heat the olive oil in a frying pan over medium heat, add the onion and garlic and cook until translucent. Stir in the cumin, coriander and lemon juice, then remove from the heat and set aside.

4 In the last half hour of cooking the broad beans, mix in the seasoning and season with salt and pepper. The beans should be very soft, but still holding their shape.

5 To serve, place the broad beans in a shallow bowl and the parsley, onion, tomato and lemon wedges on a platter alongside. Drizzle extra virgin olive oil over the beans, sprinkle with some ground cumin and serve with flatbread.

Green beans braised in olive oil

LUBIYA BI TAMATIM WA ZEIT

This simple yet tasty green bean dish is great as part of a *mezze* platter or simply served with crusty bread. It also works well as a side dish with roasted meats.

=== SERVES 4 ===

¼ cup (60 ml) olive oil
½ onion, finely chopped
2 cloves garlic, finely chopped
300 g green beans, topped,
   tailed and halved
2 tomatoes, roughly chopped

1 teaspoon baharat (see page 7)
½ teaspoon sweet paprika
½ cup (125 ml) vegetable stock
½ cup (125 ml) water
salt and freshly ground black pepper

1 Heat the olive oil in a saucepan over high heat and fry the onion and garlic for about 2 minutes. Add the beans and fry for a further 2 minutes, stirring constantly.

2 Add the tomato, baharat, paprika, stock and water and place a lid on the saucepan. Reduce the heat to a gentle simmer and cook for 30 minutes or until the beans have softened and fully absorbed the flavours. Season with salt and pepper to taste.

3 Serve warm or cold.

Red lentil soup

ADIS

When it's winter, I can't think of a better dish to keep me warm. This recipe is based on my Egyptian grandmother's recipe, but has some Turkish elements as well, such as the use of paprika and lemon juice. I can still picture my grandmother making this soup when she stayed with us in Sydney many years ago. Enjoy it with some crusty bread.

——— SERVES 4 ———

1½ cups (300 g) red lentils
60 g butter
1 onion, roughly chopped
2 cloves garlic, peeled and quartered
1 carrot, peeled and roughly chopped
1 potato, peeled and cut into 1 cm cubes
½ stick celery, thickly sliced

1 tablespoon paprika
1 teaspoon ground cumin
1 teaspoon salt
½ teaspoon freshly ground black pepper
1 litre vegetable stock
¼ cup (60 ml) lemon juice, strained
crusty bread, to serve

1 Soak the lentils in cold water for 30 minutes, then rinse and drain.

2 Melt the butter in a large saucepan over high heat, then add the onion, garlic, carrot, potato and celery and cook for about 5–8 minutes, until the vegetables start to sweat. Add the soaked lentils, paprika, cumin, salt and pepper and mix well to combine. Cook for about 2 minutes while stirring, then add the stock and bring to the boil. Boil for 2–3 minutes over high heat, then place a lid on the saucepan, reduce the heat to low and simmer gently for 1 hour. Remove from the heat and add the lemon juice.

3 Using a food processor or a stick mixer, blend the soup until smooth. Serve hot with crusty bread.

Soy bean paste stew

DWANGJANG CHIJAE

This is my favourite Korean stew, but it is an acquired taste for anyone who is not used to the pungent fermented soy bean flavour. I encourage you to give it a try – it's delicious. It is traditionally cooked with tofu in a small clay vessel that naturally helps the sauce thicken and the flavours develop. It is great to eat with a bowl of freshly steamed rice and kimchi on the side.

=== SERVES 4 ===

½ onion, thinly sliced

70 g dwangjang paste (see page 11)

1 teaspoon kochukaru (Korean chilli powder; see page 12)

1 red chilli, seeded and finely sliced

2 cloves garlic, minced

2 cups (500 ml) water

200 g firm tofu, cut into 2 cm cubes

1 zucchini (courgette), cut into 5 mm thick slices

2 spring onions, trimmed and thinly sliced on the diagonal

salt

50 g enoki mushrooms

1 extra red chilli, sliced, to garnish

1 green chilli, sliced, to garnish

steamed rice and kimchi, to serve (optional)

1 Combine the onion, dwangjang paste, kochukaru, chilli, garlic and water in a heavy-based saucepan or (preferably) a terracotta or clay pot. Stir until the dwangjang paste is diluted.

2 Bring to the boil over high heat and cook for 2 minutes, then reduce the heat to a gentle simmer. Add the tofu and cook for 5 minutes, then add the zucchini and half of the spring onion. Season with salt, then cook for a further 5 minutes, until the vegetables are tender.

3 Garnish with the mushrooms, remaining spring onion and extra red chilli and green chilli, and serve hot with steamed rice and kimchi, if you like.

Stuffed vine leaves

WARA EINAB

Wara einab is one of those dishes where you watch your lovingly rolled creation being completely devoured within minutes. The herbs add a great dimension of flavour.

=== MAKES ABOUT 20–30 ===

300 g preserved vine leaves (available from Middle Eastern and Greek grocers)

1½ cups (300 g) short-grain rice

small handful of flat-leaf parsley, leaves picked

small handful of mint, leaves picked

small bunch of dill, fronds picked

1 clove garlic, peeled

½ onion, roughly chopped

2 ripe tomatoes, roughly chopped

1 teaspoon baharat (see page 7)

½ teaspoon ground cinnamon

1 teaspoon salt

olive oil, to grease

1½ onions (extra), sliced into 1 cm thick rings

2 ripe tomatoes (extra), thinly sliced

COOKING BROTH

¼ cup (60 ml) olive oil

¼ cup (60 ml) lemon juice, strained

1 litre vegetable stock

½ teaspoon salt

¼ teaspoon freshly ground black pepper

4 cloves garlic, halved

1 Soak the vine leaves in a large bowl of warm water for 30 minutes, then rinse under cold running water and drain in a colander. (This removes the brine.) Soak the rice in a large bowl of cold water for 30 minutes, then transfer to a sieve and rinse under cold running water until the water runs clear. Set aside to drain.

2 Place the herbs, garlic, onion and tomato in a food processor and process until very finely chopped. Place the mixture in a sieve over a bowl and press down gently to remove as much liquid as possible. Reserve the liquid in the bowl.

3 Place the strained herbs and vegetables, baharat, cinnamon, salt and the drained rice in a bowl and mix well. Set aside.

4 To make the cooking broth, combine all the ingredients with the reserved strained vegetable liquid in a large bowl and mix well. Set aside.

5 Take one vine leaf, smooth-side down, with the stem facing you and the tip of the leaf away from you. Gently remove the hard stem using a knife or scissors. Place ½–1 teaspoon of the rice mixture close to the bottom end of the leaf and spread horizontally. Wrap the vine leaf tightly into a cigar shape and gently squeeze the roll. Repeat the process until all the rice mixture and vine leaves have been used.

6 Lightly oil the bottom of a deep, heavy-based casserole dish, then arrange the sliced onion in a layer over the base, followed by the sliced tomato. Pack the stuffed vine leaves tightly into the dish and gently pour the cooking broth over the top. Place a heavy, heatproof plate on top to prevent the vine leaves from unrolling, then cover the dish with the lid.

7 Bring to the boil over high heat and boil for 5 minutes, then reduce the heat to medium–low, making sure the lid remains tightly closed. Cook for 1½ hours, checking every 20 minutes or so that there is still enough cooking broth. If the broth becomes low, add ½ cup (125 ml) of water at a time, along with a pinch of salt.

8 Allow the stuffed vine leaves to cool, then serve either warm or cold.

Pickled cabbage

BAECHU KIMCHI

When someone talks about Korean food, the immediate association is kimchi! 'Kimchi' literally means fermenting or pickling. This recipe is for *baechu kimchi*, the famous wombok (Chinese cabbage or *baechu* in Korean) kimchi. Eman and I would always know when Mum was making kimchi, as the smell of pickling cabbage, mixed with the aromas of garlic and ginger would waft through the house. Making kimchi is quite a long process, but having freshly made kimchi is well worth the wait, as once you have it in your fridge you can use it for lots of different recipes.

=== MAKES ABOUT 1 KG ===

1 large wombok (Chinese cabbage), base trimmed and any damaged outer leaves removed, cut in half lengthways
¾ cup (215 g) coarse cooking salt

FILLING
½ daikon, cut into thin 5 cm batons
50 g Chinese/Korean chives (see page 7), cut into 3 cm lengths
8 cloves garlic, minced
20 g ginger, minced
4 spring onions, trimmed and sliced into 3 cm lengths on the diagonal
⅓ cup (80 g) kochukaru (Korean chilli powder; see page 12)
½ cup (125 ml) water
¼ cup (70 g) myulchi aekjot (Korean fish sauce; see page 12)
1 teaspoon salt

1 Open the leaves of the cabbage halves and spread the salt evenly between the layers. Allow to sit for 4 hours, turning the cabbage every hour. Rinse the cabbage under cold running water several times, then leave to drain in a colander for 2 hours.

2 To make the filling, place all the ingredients in a large bowl and mix well. Take one half of the cabbage and, using your hands, stuff the filling in between the layers of the cabbage leaves. Repeat the process with the other half of the cabbage. Coat the entire cabbage with the filling.

3 Tightly pack both cabbage halves into a clean, dry airtight container. Leave at room temperature overnight, then refrigerate for 2 days.

4 Serve as a side dish to Korean meals or use as part of a recipe requiring kimchi.

5 The kimchi can be stored in the fridge for up to 3 months.

Korean buckwheat noodle salad

BIBIMGUKSU

In summer, my sister and I love making this salad, quickly chopping the fresh vegetables and dressing it all with a hot, sweet sauce. The resulting dish is as healthy and refreshing to eat as it is quick and easy to make.

=== SERVES 4 ===

1 cucumber, seeded and cut into
    5 cm matchsticks
1 carrot, peeled and cut into 5 cm
    matchsticks
¼ iceberg lettuce, thinly shredded
¼ red onion, thinly sliced
1 nashi pear, peeled and cut into
    5 cm matchsticks
200 g naeng myun noodles (see page 12)
2 hard-boiled eggs, peeled and halved
small ice cubes (optional)

DRESSING
1 tablespoon sesame seeds
⅓ cup (80 ml) gochujang (Korean
    hot pepper paste; see page 11)
1 teaspoon kochukaru (Korean
    chilli powder; see page 12)
2 tablespoons sesame oil
2 teaspoons dark soy sauce
2 tablespoons sugar
2 tablespoons apple cider vinegar
2 tablespoons water

1 Place the cucumber, carrot, lettuce, onion and pear in separate bowls in the fridge.

2 To make the dressing, toast the sesame seeds in a dry frying pan over medium heat for about 3 minutes, until fragrant and golden. Place all the remaining ingredients in a small bowl and mix well. Add the toasted sesame seeds and mix to combine.

3 Bring a large saucepan of water to the boil, then add the noodles, stir immediately and cook for about 3–4 minutes, until they are al dente, still with a slight bite. Transfer the noodles to a colander and rinse them under cold running water several times until all the starch has been removed and the noodles have completely cooled. Leave to drain.

4 Divide the noodles among four plates or bowls. Arrange the pear and vegetables around the noodles, then place an egg half on top. Drizzle some of the dressing over the noodles, then garnish with three or four small ice cubes to keep the dish cool, if you like. Serve immediately before the noodles stick together.

Stir-fried Korean noodles with vegetables

JAPCHAE

Every Korean mother I know has her own version of *japchae*. My mum has always made it a vegetarian dish, but you could fry strips of beef fillet with soy sauce and garlic, then add the meat to the noodle mix towards the end if you like. Dang myun noodles are unique to Korean cuisine, making this dish even more special.

=== SERVES 4–6 ===

300 g dang myun noodles (see page 11)
¼ cup (60 ml) vegetable oil
1 onion, thinly sliced
1 carrot, peeled and cut into
   5 cm matchsticks
1 red capsicum (pepper), seeds and
   membrane discarded, cut into thin strips
10 fresh shiitake mushrooms, thinly sliced
¼ cup (60 ml) soy sauce

100 g baby spinach
½ teaspoon salt
¼ cup (60 ml) sesame oil
2 tablespoons sesame seeds
1 spring onion, trimmed and
   sliced on the diagonal
1 clove garlic, minced
1 tablespoon sugar
salt and freshly ground black pepper

1 Cook the dang myun noodles in a large saucepan of boiling water for about 4–5 minutes, until tender, then transfer to a colander and rinse under cold running water until cool. Drain and set aside.

2 Heat 1 tablespoon of vegetable oil in a frying pan over medium heat and cook the onion for about 3 minutes, until softened and fragrant, then transfer to a medium bowl and set aside.

3 Heat another tablespoon of vegetable oil in the same frying pan over medium heat and stir-fry the carrot and capsicum together for a few minutes, until slightly softened and vibrant in colour. Add to the bowl of cooked onion.

4 Heat the remaining vegetable oil in the frying pan over medium heat and fry the mushrooms for 1 minute, then add 1 tablespoon of soy sauce and cook for a further 2 minutes, until the mushrooms start to soften. Add to the bowl.

5 Blanch the spinach for 1 minute in a saucepan of salted boiling water, then drain and rinse under cold running water. Squeeze out any excess liquid from the spinach using your hands. When cool, transfer to a separate bowl and stir in the salt and 1 tablespoon of sesame oil, mixing well. Set aside.

6 Toast the sesame seeds in a dry frying pan over medium heat for about 3 minutes, until fragrant and golden.

7 Transfer the noodles, all the cooked vegetables and the spring onion to a large bowl. Stir in the toasted sesame seeds, garlic, sugar and remaining soy sauce and sesame oil, mixing well to ensure the noodles and vegetables are thoroughly coated with the dressing. Season with salt and pepper to taste and serve warm.

Korean rice cakes

TTEOKBOKKI

Tteokbokki is a famous street food in Korea. People buy these soft spicy rice cakes from street vendors, who also offer fish cake soup to calm the tastebuds from all the spiciness. When Mum and I are keen for a quick and easy lunch at home, this is one of our favourites. The garatteok are available from Korean stores, and it is best to use the fresh ones.

=== SERVES 4 ===

1½ cups (375 ml) water
½ onion, thinly sliced
1 clove garlic, minced
1½ tablespoons gochujang (Korean hot pepper paste; see page 12)
1 tablespoon kochukaru (Korean chilli powder; see page 12)
1 teaspoon soy sauce
1 tablespoon sesame oil
1 tablespoon vegetable oil

250 g garatteok (rice cakes), cut into 5 cm pieces
1 tablespoon sugar
3 wombok (Chinese cabbage) leaves, roughly chopped
½ large carrot, peeled and cut into thin 5 cm batons
1 spring onion, trimmed and sliced into 2 cm lengths on the diagonal

1 Place the water, onion, garlic, gochujang, kochukaru, soy sauce, sesame oil and vegetable oil in a shallow saucepan and cook over high heat for about 3 minutes, stirring well, until the gochujang is completely dissolved. Bring to the boil, then after 3 minutes reduce the heat to a gentle simmer and add the rice cakes.

2 Gently simmer the rice cakes in the sauce for 10 minutes, stirring regularly so that they do not stick to the pan. Add the sugar, cabbage, carrot and spring onion and cook for a further 5 minutes. Serve hot.

Mixed vegetables and rice

BIBIMPAP

Bibimpap is taking the world by storm. With its delicious seasoned vegetables, spicy chilli sauce and runny egg, it is being hailed as a new 'wellbeing food'.

———— SERVES 4 ————

2 cups (400 g) short-grain rice
2½ cups (625 ml) water
2 tablespoons sesame seeds
⅓ cup (80 ml) vegetable oil
12 shiitake mushrooms, thinly sliced
salt
1 carrot, peeled and cut into 5 cm batons
1 large zucchini (courgette), halved
  lengthways and thinly sliced
150 g English spinach, stalks removed
2¼ tablespoons sesame oil
150 g soy bean sprouts, roots trimmed,
  washed and drained
2 tablespoons apple cider vinegar
1 clove garlic, minced

1 tablespoon kochukaru (Korean
  chilli powder; see page 12)
½ daikon, cut into thin 5 cm batons
4 eggs
¼ iceberg lettuce, thinly shredded
50 g toasted seaweed (see page 12),
  thinly shredded

DRESSING
2 tablespoons gochujang (Korean
  hot pepper paste; see page 12)
1 tablespoon sugar
1 tablespoon water
1 tablespoon apple cider vinegar
1 tablespoon sesame oil
1 clove garlic, minced

1 Wash the rice under cold water until the water runs clear, then place it in a heavy-based saucepan and add the water. Cook over high heat for 5 minutes, until the water boils, then for a further 2 minutes. Cover with a tight-fitting lid, reduce the heat to low and cook for 20 minutes. Remove from the heat and keep covered for 10 minutes. Fluff the rice with a fork.

2 To make the dressing, place all the ingredients in a small bowl and mix well. Set aside.

3 Toast the sesame seeds in a dry frying pan over medium heat for about 3 minutes, until fragrant and golden. Transfer to a small bowl and set aside.

4 Heat 1 tablespoon of vegetable oil in a frying pan over high heat and stir-fry the mushrooms, lightly seasoned with salt, for 2 minutes. Transfer to a bowl. Repeat with another tablespoon of oil to cook the carrot and then more oil and the zucchini.

5 Blanch the spinach for 1 minute in salted boiling water, then drain and rinse under cold water. Squeeze out any excess liquid and leave to cool, then transfer the spinach to a bowl and stir in 1 tablespoon of sesame oil and ½ teaspoon of salt.

6 Steam the soy bean sprouts, covered, over boiling water for 3 minutes. Remove and allow to cool, then mix in 1 tablespoon of sesame oil and ½ teaspoon of salt and set aside.

7 In a small bowl, combine the vinegar with the remaining sesame oil, garlic, kochukaru and 1 teaspoon of salt. Add the daikon, mix well and set aside.

8 Heat the remaining vegetable oil in a frying pan over medium heat, then fry the eggs, two at a time, for about 3 minutes, until the whites are set but the yolks are still runny.

9 To assemble, divide the rice among four bowls, then arrange the cooked vegetables, lettuce and toasted seaweed neatly on top. Place one egg on top of each bowl. Drizzle with dressing, then sprinkle with toasted sesame seeds. Serve warm.

CLOCKWISE FROM TOP:

RICE WITH VERMICELLI P 81
SAFFRON RICE P 83
JEWELLED COUSCOUS P 82

Rice with vermicelli

ROZ BI SHA'RIYYAH

Egg vermicelli made into round parcels are a staple in every Egyptian household. The fried vermicelli adds a mild nutty flavour to any dish and, quite frankly, is also scrumptious on its own. It is a great accompaniment to a saucy stew.

====== SERVES 4 ======

2¼ cups (450 g) long-grain rice
40 g butter
120 g egg vermicelli pasta, roughly crushed
  into 2–3 cm pieces

1 teaspoon salt
½ teaspoon freshly ground black pepper
1 litre boiling water or chicken stock

1 Rinse the rice under cold water, drain and repeat several times.

2 Melt the butter in a heavy-based saucepan over medium heat, then stir through the vermicelli and cook for about 3 minutes, until golden-brown. Add the rice and stir until the grains are glistening.

3 Add the salt and pepper, then the boiling water or stock. Stir quickly once, then bring to the boil. Stretch a clean tea towel over the top of the saucepan and place a tight-fitting lid on top. Fold the edges of the tea towel up over the lid. Reduce the heat to a gentle simmer and cook for 25 minutes, never opening the lid.

4 Remove the saucepan from the heat and allow the rice to rest in the covered saucepan for 10 minutes. Remove the saucepan lid and tea towel, give the rice a gentle fluff with a fork, then serve.

Jewelled couscous

Couscous is a versatile grain that features widely in Moroccan cooking. It is a fabulous addition to a tagine or flavoursome stew, as it absorbs sauces very easily. This dish is great with simple or grilled protein dishes that are not too heavily flavoured and is also a lovely salad on its own. *Pictured page 80.*

=== SERVES 4 ===

¼ cup (40 g) pine nuts
¼ cup (35 g) slivered almonds
1½ cups (300 g) couscous
¼ cup (35 g) raw shelled pistachios, chopped
¼ cup (40 g) currants

1 teaspoon ground cinnamon
1 teaspoon ground cumin
½ teaspoon ground cardamom
1 teaspoon salt
50 g butter, chopped
1 cup (250 ml) water

1 Preheat the oven to 180°C. Spread the pine nuts over a baking tray and toast in the oven for about 5 minutes, until golden-brown, shaking the tray occasionally so they don't burn. Repeat the same process for the almonds.

2 Place the couscous in a large bowl and add the pistachios, currants and toasted pine nuts and almonds. Set aside.

3 Place the spices, salt, butter and water in a saucepan and bring to the boil, then remove from the heat and gently pour over the couscous. Do not stir. Quickly cover the bowl tightly with plastic film to prevent steam from escaping and leave for 5 minutes.

4 Using a fork, mix all the ingredients together until well combined, fluffing up the grains of couscous as you go. Serve warm.

Saffron rice

ROZ BI ZA'FARAN

Saffron is truly an extraordinary spice. It has had so much influence throughout history, especially in regards to the spice trade. In this recipe, it gives the rice grains a beautiful hue and aroma. This makes a lovely accompaniment for grilled meats. *Pictured page 80.*

=== SERVES 4 ===

2 cups (400 g) basmati rice
1 tablespoon salt
40 g butter
10 saffron threads

½ teaspoon salt (extra)
1 litre boiling vegetable stock

1 Soak the rice for an hour in cold water with 1 tablespoon of salt. Rinse the rice several times, then leave to drain in a colander for 15 minutes.

2 Melt the butter in a large heavy-based saucepan over medium heat. Add the saffron and cook for 30 seconds, then add the rice and stir thoroughly to coat the grains with the saffron mixture.

3 Stir in the extra salt, then add the boiling stock. Stir quickly once, then bring to the boil. Stretch a clean tea towel over the top of the saucepan and place a tight-fitting lid on top. Fold the edges of the tea towel up over the lid. Reduce the heat to a gentle simmer and cook for 20 minutes, never opening the lid.

4 Remove the saucepan from the heat and allow the rice to rest in the covered saucepan for 10 minutes. Remove the saucepan lid and tea towel, give the rice a good fluff with a fork, then serve.

Lentil rice

KOSHARI

This is a much-loved Egyptian dish, wholesome and full of flavour. In Egypt, it is easy to find a stall or shop specialising in *koshari*, so it is a popular and cheap option when you're out and about. This is a fabulous dish for vegetarians, but everyone will enjoy it.

=== SERVES 6 ===

Rice with vermicelli (see page 81)
200 g small elbow macaroni
2 cups (500 ml) vegetable oil
2 onions, very thinly sliced

SPICED LENTILS
500 g green lentils, soaked for 1 hour
½ cup (125 ml) olive oil
1 onion, halved and then thinly sliced
3 cloves garlic, finely chopped
½ bunch coriander, leaves and stems
  finely chopped
1 tablespoon ground cumin
1 tablespoon ground coriander
½ cup (125 ml) water
salt

TOMATO SAUCE
1 tablespoon olive oil
2 cloves garlic, finely chopped
3 cups (780 g) passata
¼ cup (60 ml) white vinegar
1 teaspoon ground cumin
1 teaspoon chilli powder
½ teaspoon salt

1 To make the spiced lentils, rinse the lentils a few times, then place them in a saucepan and cover with twice as much cold water. Bring to the boil over high heat, then reduce the heat and cook for 15 minutes until the lentils are tender, but still retain their shape. Drain the lentils and set aside.

2 Heat the olive oil in a large frying pan over medium heat and fry the onion, garlic and chopped coriander until softened and fragrant, about 3 minutes. Add the cumin and coriander, then stir in the lentils. Pour in the water and stir gently over the heat for a further 2 minutes. Season with salt, then remove the pan from the heat.

3 To make the tomato sauce, heat the olive oil in a saucepan over high heat and fry the garlic for 2 minutes, until fragrant and golden, being careful not to burn it. Add the remaining ingredients and bring to the boil, then reduce the heat to low and simmer, covered, for 20 minutes. Remove from the heat.

4 While the tomato sauce is simmering, cook the macaroni in a saucepan of boiling water until al dente. Drain and set aside.

5 Pour the vegetable oil into a large saucepan and heat until it registers 180°C on a thermometer (or a cube of bread dropped into the oil browns in 20 seconds). Fry the onion, in small batches, for 2–3 minutes, until just golden-brown and crispy. Remove with a slotted spoon and drain on paper towels.

6 To assemble, place some rice with vermicelli in six shallow dishes and top with the pasta and lentils. Add a few spoonfuls of the tomato sauce, then garnish with the fried onion. Serve warm.

SEAFOOD

SEAFOOD

This delicate and intriguing category of proteins is much loved by my family. Here in Sydney, my parents have visited the Sydney Fish Market every weekend for years, purchasing only the freshest seafood to recreate their much-loved Korean and Egyptian dishes. No matter how many times my parents visit the market, there are two types of seafood they will always buy – silver bream and prawns.

Korea is largely surrounded by water, and the seafood dishes vary according to the produce of the particular region. A common delicacy, especially in fishing ports such as Busan and the beautiful island of Jeju, is freshly caught filleted fish and crustaceans, served raw with traditional gochujang sauce slightly acidified with vinegar. Korea has amazing seafood markets in the larger cities, generally run by women who will, on request, provide helpful cooking advice.

Although most of Egypt is inland, some well-known seaside locations such as Alexandria, Port Said and the Suez Canal are renowned for their seafood dishes. Dad is from Alexandria, which is known for its charcoaled grey mullet (see page 102). To this day you will still find seafood vendors at the fish markets there, selling their grilled fish wrapped in newspaper ready to be purchased and enjoyed at home.

Most of the recipes in this chapter are either traditional Korean or Egyptian dishes, but some are a combination of the two. Garlic and chilli prawns (page 90), Very hot crab (page 92) and Sumac-crusted trout (page 108) are recipes I have experimented with, integrating elements of both cuisines – fortunately, my family love them.

Garlic and chilli prawns

GAMBARI BI TOMB WA FILFIL HARR

My family has always enjoyed good, old-fashioned garlic prawns. However, on a recent trip to Spain, Eman and I discovered this tapas version and I haven't looked back since. This recipe is far more delicious than the traditional version, especially when served with crusty bread. I have used verjuice here, as I find it adds a subtle sweetness and acidity to the dish.

——— SERVES 4 ———

500 g green (raw) king prawns,
   peeled and deveined, tails intact
2 tablespoons olive oil
3 cloves garlic, minced
1 red chilli, seeded and finely sliced
2 tablespoons verjuice

1 teaspoon butter
1 tablespoon finely chopped
   flat-leaf parsley (optional)
¼ teaspoon salt
crusty bread, to serve (optional)

1 Pat the prawns dry with paper towels to remove any excess moisture.

2 Heat the olive oil in a frying pan over high heat, add the garlic and fry for 1 minute, then add the chilli and stir for just 30 seconds to make sure the garlic does not burn. Add the prawns and stir for 1 minute, then add the verjuice and cook for another 2 minutes. The prawns should be pink, but remain supple.

3 Stir in the butter, parsley (if using) and salt and cook for another minute. Remove from the heat and serve immediately with crusty bread, if you like.

Very hot crab!

Mum and Eman have a super-tolerance to very hot food, and one day Mum came back from the fish markets with some crabs and asked if I could cook them in a spicy sauce. I put these flavours together and they loved it! It is hilarious seeing Mum and Eman trying to deal with the heat of the dish, yet wanting more of the sauce. You could use two large mud crabs, divided into six pieces each, instead of blue swimmer crabs if you like.

=== SERVES 4 ===

½ cup (125 ml) vegetable oil
4 blue swimmer crabs, cleaned,
    quartered and claws gently cracked
    with the back of a large knife
½ cup (125 ml) water
kaffir lime leaves, to garnish
sliced red chilli, to garnish
handful of coriander leaves, to garnish
    (optional)
steamed rice, to serve (optional)

SPICE PASTE
⅓ cup (80 ml) white vinegar
¼ cup (60 ml) lime juice
¼ cup (60 ml) water
4 red chillies, seeded and quartered
4 dried chillies (see page 11), rehydrated
    in hot water for 30 minutes
3 golden shallots, peeled and quartered
2 tablespoons grated palm sugar
1 tablespoon tomato paste (puree)
3 cloves garlic, peeled
1 × 2 cm piece ginger, quartered
2 kaffir lime leaves
1 teaspoon salt

1 To make the spice paste, place all the ingredients in a food processor, and blitz until well combined. Set aside.

2 Heat the vegetable oil in a wok over high heat until very hot, then add the crabs, in batches, and fry for 2 minutes. Remove from the wok.

3 Add the spice paste and fry over medium heat for 2 minutes, until fragrant, then add the crabs and water and cook for a further 5 minutes. The crabs should have changed colour and the sauce will have thickened.

4 Remove the crabs from the wok and garnish with kaffir lime leaves, sliced red chilli and coriander, if using. Serve immediately with steamed rice, if you like.

Slow-braised baby octopus

UKHTUBUT BI TAMATIM

This recipe is perfect for the winter months. Baby octopus can be prepared in many ways, but gentle slow cooking is the key to making it tender, and this is especially important here. Enjoy this dish with crusty bread to soak up the aromatic sauce.

=== SERVES 4 ===

¼ cup (60 ml) olive oil
4 small onions, peeled and quartered
2 cloves garlic, minced
2 bay leaves
2 tablespoons finely chopped
   flat-leaf parsley, plus extra to garnish
1 tablespoon oregano leaves,
   finely chopped
1 kg baby octopus, cleaned
   and beaks removed

½ cup (125 ml) verjuice
2 cups (520 g) passata
3 ripe tomatoes, roughly chopped
1 cup (250 ml) fish stock
1 teaspoon salt
½ teaspoon freshly ground black pepper
crusty bread, to serve

1 Heat the olive oil in a large heavy-based casserole dish over medium heat. When hot, add the onion and garlic and cook for 2 minutes, until fragrant. Add the bay leaves, parsley, oregano and octopus and cook for 3 minutes, stirring, then add the verjuice, passata, tomato, stock, salt and pepper.

2 Bring to the boil and boil for 2 minutes, then cover tightly with a lid, reduce the heat to a gentle simmer and braise for 1½ hours. The octopus should be tender and flavoursome.

3 Garnish with extra parsley and serve immediately with crusty bread.

Stir-fried squid

OJINGOH BOKKUM

Koreans love using squid in their cuisine. This particular fresh squid dish is fiery to the palate, so if you are not a huge chilli fan, perhaps cut down the amount of gochujang and kochukaru. Cook this quickly, as you don't want to overcook the squid. It is best served with hot steamed rice.

=== SERVES 4 ===

300 g squid tubes, cleaned (ask your
    fishmonger to do this for you)
2 tablespoons vegetable oil
1 carrot, peeled and cut into thin batons
2 large wombok (Chinese cabbage) leaves,
    thinly shredded
1 onion, thinly sliced
sesame seeds, to garnish
steamed rice, to serve

SAUCE
1 tablespoon gochujang (Korean hot
    pepper paste; see page 12)
1 tablespoon sesame oil
1 tablespoon dark soy sauce
1 tablespoon rice vinegar
1 tablespoon water
1 clove garlic, minced
1 teaspoon kochukaru (Korean chilli
    powder; see page 12)
1 teaspoon white sugar

1 Cut the squid tubes in half lengthways and score the backs in a criss-cross pattern at 5 mm intervals. Cut into bite-sized pieces.

2 To make the sauce, mix all the ingredients together in a bowl and set aside.

3 Heat the vegetable oil in a wok over high heat, then add the carrot, cabbage and onion and fry for 1 minute. Add the squid and fry for 1 minute more. Add the sauce and stir to coat the squid and vegetables. Cook for a further 2 minutes, until the squid is cooked through but still tender.

4 Garnish with sesame seeds and serve immediately with steamed rice.

Baked fish with tahini and chilli

SAMAKA HARRA BI TAHINA WA FILFIL

This is perhaps the most famous method of cooking fish in the northern region of the Middle East. The mixture of creamy tahini sauce, crunchy pine nuts, a kick of heat and the tart lemon finish makes this dish a flavour sensation. I recommend using a white-fleshed fish, such as snapper, red emperor or barramundi.

=== SERVES 4 ===

½ cup (80 g) pine nuts
2 tablespoons olive oil
2 tablespoons lemon juice
1 teaspoon salt
1 whole snapper (about 1.5 kg),
    gilled, gutted and scaled (ask your
    fishmonger to do this for you)
olive oil (extra), for oiling
handful of roughly chopped flat-leaf parsley
steamed rice, to serve

TAHINI AND CHILLI SAUCE
¾ cup (210 g) tahini
½ cup (125 ml) lemon juice, strained
1¼ cups (310 ml) water
2 cloves garlic, minced
1 teaspoon salt
1 teaspoon chilli flakes

1 Preheat the oven to 180°C. Spread the pine nuts over a baking tray and toast in the oven for about 5 minutes, until golden-brown, shaking the tray occasionally so they don't burn. Remove from the oven and set aside.

2 Combine the olive oil, lemon juice and salt in a small bowl.

3 Cut three shallow slits in each side of the fish, then place it in a deep baking dish lightly oiled with extra olive oil. Pour half of the lemon juice mixture over the fish, rubbing it in with your fingers, and pour the rest inside the fish.

4 Bake for 20 minutes, then turn the fish over and bake for a further 15 minutes or until cooked through. To test if the fish is done, insert a fork into the thickest part of the flesh – if the fork goes through easily, it is ready.

5 While the fish is baking, make the tahini and chilli sauce. Place all the ingredients in a small bowl and whisk together with a balloon whisk or stick mixer until it is smooth and free of lumps. If the mixture is too thick, whisk in a few teaspoons of water until it is the consistency of pancake batter.

6 Once the fish is cooked, remove it from the oven and carefully pour the tahini and chilli sauce over the top. Return it to the oven for 5 minutes.

7 Remove the fish from the oven, sprinkle with toasted pine nuts and garnish with parsley. Serve immediately with steamed rice.

Deep-fried whitebait

SAMAK BIZRI BI LAYMOON WA KAMOUN

Whitebait is an under-used fish, but I hope this recipe will show you just how easy it is to prepare. This recipe is from Alexandria, Egypt, and I have added a little more spice to jazz it up. I clearly remember my father making this when I was a little girl and eating the whitebait straight away with lots of lemon juice before the dish even reached the table. The whitebait looks great served in newspaper cones with lemon cheeks.

—— SERVES 4 ——

400 g whitebait
1 cup (150 g) plain flour
½ teaspoon ground cumin
½ teaspoon ground coriander
¼ teaspoon cayenne pepper

¾ teaspoon salt
¼ teaspoon freshly ground black pepper
1 litre vegetable oil
lemon cheeks, to serve

1 Wash the whitebait in a colander under cold running water, then leave to drain for 10 minutes.

2 Combine the flour, spices, salt and pepper in a large bowl and mix well. Add the whitebait in three batches and toss to coat, shaking off the excess.

3 Heat the vegetable oil in a large saucepan over high heat until it registers 180°C on a thermometer (or until a cube of bread dropped into the oil browns in 20 seconds). Add the first batch of whitebait to the hot oil and stir gently to avoid clumping. Cook until crunchy and golden-brown, then remove with a slotted spoon and drain on a plate lined with paper towels. Repeat with the remaining whitebait, reheating the oil between batches.

4 Serve the whitebait piping hot, with lemon cheeks alongside.

Charcoaled grey mullet

SAMAK MASHWI

In the Egyptian city of Alexandria, the fish markets are located right on the waterfront. The locals shop there every day for their fresh fish and many take their purchases to nearby restaurants that specialise in cooking seafood on charcoal. My family take this option when buying their seafood, not only to make it easier but also because the charcoal barbecues add an incredibly delicious flavour.

Charcoaled grey mullet is a specialty of Alexandria and much loved by the locals. The wheatgerm allows the fish's skin to blacken from the coals, while protecting the delicate white meat, as well as infusing smokiness throughout.

=========== SERVES 4–6 ===========

1 cup (100 g) wheatgerm
¼ cup (60 g) fine salt
2 large grey mullet (roughly 1.5 kg each), gilled, gutted and scaled (ask your fishmonger to do this for you)

1 cup (250 ml) lemon juice, strained
1 tablespoon ground cumin
1 teaspoon fine salt (extra)
salad and steamed rice, to serve (optional)

1 First, heat a charcoal barbecue until the charcoals are white in colour. (If you do not have a charcoal barbecue, you can use a gas barbecue, however the flavour will not be the same.)

2 Combine the wheatgerm and ¼ cup (55 g) of salt in a large tray. Rinse the fish under cold running water, then lightly shake it to remove some of the water. Add the fish, one at a time, to the wheatgerm mixture, tossing to coat well, then press the wheatgerm mixture into the skin of the fish.

3 Place the coated mullets inside a very large hinged wire basket for fish and place the basket onto the preheated charcoal barbecue. Cook on one side for 15 minutes, followed by a further 15 minutes on the other side.

4 While the fish is cooking, combine the lemon juice, cumin and 1 teaspoon of extra salt in a small bowl.

5 Transfer each fish to a large piece of foil. Spoon the lemon juice mixture equally over each fish, then wrap the foil tightly around the fish. Rest for 10 minutes.

6 Serve with salad and rice on the side if you like.

Red mullet with tomatoes and onion

BARBOUNIA FIL FORN

My uncle's wife, Fatimah, made this dish many years ago when she invited my family over for dinner during our travels in Egypt. I loved the flavour of the mullet infused with the spiced tomato sauce, as well as the tenderness that comes with baking it. Serve this straight out of the oven when it is piping hot, and watch out for the tiny bones.

===== SERVES 4 =====

2 tablespoons olive oil
2 white onions, thinly sliced
1 kg small red mullet, gilled, gutted
    and scaled (ask your fishmonger
    to do this for you)
2 tomatoes, thinly sliced

SAUCE
2 cups (500 ml) fish or vegetable stock
⅓ cup (80 ml) lemon juice
2 tablespoons roughly chopped
    flat-leaf parsley
2 cloves garlic, finely chopped
1 teaspoon baharat (see page 7)
1 teaspoon ground cumin
salt and freshly ground black pepper

1 Preheat the oven to 190°C.

2 To make the sauce, place all the ingredients in a saucepan and bring to the boil over high heat. Reduce the heat to medium and simmer for 2 minutes, stirring until the spices have dissolved. Remove from the heat and set aside.

3 Add the olive oil to a shallow baking tin or ovenproof dish and spread it over the bottom. Layer the onion rings on top and then place the mullet on top of the onion. Layer the sliced tomato over the fish, then gently pour the sauce over the top.

4 Transfer to the oven and cook, uncovered, for 30 minutes. Serve immediately.

Sardine kofta tagine

TAGIINE BI SARDIN

In Morocco, it is not unusual to see fishermen in their boats making this on a portable stove and sharing it with each other, perhaps with some bread. It is best cooked in a tagine (see page 8), however a heavy-based pan or casserole dish will also be fine. In this dish, the distinct smell and flavour of the sardines are subtly toned down by the aromatic sauce they are braised in.

=== SERVES 4 ===

strips of lemon rind, to garnish
lemon wedges and flatbread,
   to serve (optional)

SARDINE KOFTAS
600 g sardine fillets, deboned
   (ask your fishmonger to do this for you)
1 tablespoon finely chopped
   flat-leaf parsley
1 clove garlic, minced
1 teaspoon ground cumin
1 teaspoon ground coriander
1/3 teaspoon cayenne pepper
1/2 teaspoon salt

SAUCE
1/3 cup (80 ml) olive oil
1 white onion, finely chopped
2 cloves garlic, minced
2 cups (500 ml) vegetable stock
4 ripe tomatoes, chopped into small cubes
2 tablespoons tomato paste (puree)
1/2 preserved lemon, rind only, rinsed
   and thinly sliced
1 teaspoon mild paprika
1 teaspoon ground cumin
1 teaspoon salt
1/4 teaspoon freshly ground black pepper

1. To make the koftas, place the sardine fillets in a food processor and process until they are finely chopped, but not pureed or smooth.

2. Transfer the sardines to a large bowl, then add the rest of the ingredients and mix together well. Cover and refrigerate for 1 hour.

3. Meanwhile, to make the sauce, heat the olive oil in a tagine, heavy-based saucepan or flameproof casserole dish over medium heat. Add the onion and garlic and cook for about 2 minutes, until fragrant, then add the remaining ingredients. Bring to the boil over high heat, then reduce the heat to low and simmer gently for 5 minutes, stirring once to ensure the spices have dissolved.

4. Remove the sardine mixture from the fridge and form it into small balls (about 2 cm in diameter). Add the balls to the simmering sauce and stir gently to coat well. Place the lid on and simmer for 10 minutes, then stir the mixture gently and cook, covered, for a further 10 minutes.

5. Garnish with strips of lemon rind and serve immediately, with lemon wedges and flatbread, if you like.

Sumac-crusted trout with heirloom tomato salsa

My parents and Eman absolutely love salmon, but I prefer trout. This superb dish is a wonderful way to cook either. The sumac gives a light citrus finish and the acidity of the tomato salad helps to cut through the richness of the fish. I have used heirloom tomatoes in the salsa as they add a beautiful colour palette, as well as a variety of flavours.

=== SERVES 4 ===

2 tablespoons sumac
½ teaspoon salt
4 × 120–140 g ocean trout fillets, skin removed and pin-boned
2 tablespoons olive oil

HEIRLOOM TOMATO SALSA
300 g heirloom tomatoes, roughly chopped
¼ red onion, finely chopped
⅓ cup (80 ml) lemon juice, strained
⅓ cup (80 ml) extra virgin olive oil
1 tablespoon finely chopped mint
1 tablespoon finely chopped coriander
½ teaspoon salt

1 To make the salsa, place all the ingredients in a bowl and mix together well. Cover with plastic film and leave in the fridge for 30 minutes.

2 Place the sumac and salt in a large bowl and mix well. Toss each trout fillet in the sumac and salt, patting down the mixture so that the fillets are well coated.

3 Heat the olive oil in a large heavy-based frying pan over medium heat. Cook the trout fillets for 4 minutes on each side, until just cooked through.

4 Place the trout on serving plates with the tomato salsa alongside. Serve immediately.

Mackerel with daikon

GODUNGO JORIM

My mother makes this dish the same way her mother did. My *emo* (aunty) Shin Joung told me once that the vinegar in the sauce helps to reduce the strong smell of the mackerel when cooking. The daikon absorbs the flavours, adding mild sweetness and freshness to the dish.

===== SERVES 4 =====

1 × 20 cm piece daikon, peeled and cut
   into 2 cm cubes
1 kg mackerel, gilled, gutted and scaled
   (ask your fishmonger to do this for you)
1 white onion, halved and thinly sliced
2 red chillies, finely sliced
steamed rice, to serve (optional)

SAUCE
2 cups (500 ml) water
½ cup (125 ml) dark soy sauce
2 cloves garlic, minced
1 tablespoon white vinegar
1 tablespoon white sugar
1 teaspoon kochukaru (Korean chilli
   powder; see page 12)

1 To make the sauce, mix all the ingredients in a small bowl until well combined.

2 Spread the daikon over the bottom of a deep heavy-based saucepan or flameproof casserole dish.

3 Remove the head and tail of the mackerel, then slice it into 5 cm wide pieces, cutting through the spine. Place the mackerel on top of the daikon, then add the onion and chilli. Gently pour the sauce over the mackerel and vegetables.

4 Cover with a lid and cook over high heat until the stew begins to boil rapidly. Remove the lid and spoon some of the cooking liquid over the top of the mackerel. Reduce the heat to a gentle simmer and cook, covered, for a further 30 minutes, until the fish is cooked and the daikon is tender enough to cut through.

5 Serve immediately with steamed rice, if you like.

Alexandrian-style stuffed sea bream

SAMAK ISKANDARANI

This fish dish is by far the favourite of my whole family. No one will ever complain about this meal! It is so flavoursome, especially when you use your hands and pull apart the tender flesh that has absorbed the aroma and flavour of the stuffing. My mother was taught this recipe by Dad's Egyptian mother and each time she makes it the whole family gathers joyfully around the table.

===== SERVES 4 =====

4 small (around 300 g each) whole silver
    bream or deep sea bream, gilled, gutted
    and scaled (ask your fishmonger to do
    this for you)
½ cup (75 g) plain flour
1 teaspoon salt
½ teaspoon freshly ground black pepper
olive oil, for frying
lemon wedges and steamed rice,
    to serve (optional)

STUFFING
large handful of coriander stems and
    leaves, roughly chopped
4 cloves garlic, quartered
2 tablespoons lemon juice, strained
1 red chilli, seeded and finely sliced
1 teaspoon ground cumin
½ teaspoon salt

1 Rinse the fish under cold running water and leave to drain.

2 To make the stuffing, place all the ingredients in a food processor and process until finely chopped, but not a paste. Divide the stuffing into four portions and stuff the bellies of the fish.

3 Combine the flour, salt and pepper in a large shallow tray. Gently place one side of a fish at a time in the seasoned flour, patting gently to ensure the flour coats the fish. Repeat with the other side, turning carefully so the stuffing remains secure. Tap to remove any excess flour and set aside.

4 Pour enough olive oil into a large, heavy-based saucepan to reach 5 mm deep and heat over medium heat. Place two fish in the pan at a time. Cook on one side for 5 minutes, then turn the fish over and cook on the other side for a further 5–7 minutes or until just cooked. To test if the fish is done, insert a fork into the thickest part of the flesh and if the fork goes though easily, it is ready.

5 Place the fish on a large serving platter and serve immediately with lemon wedges and steamed rice, if you like.

Seafood tagine with chermoula

TAGIINE BI MA'KOOLAT BAHRIYA WA CHERMOULA

Moroccan food has many similarities to Egyptian food, in terms of the cooking methods, as well as some of the spices used. I discovered the benefits of a clay tagine many years ago (see page 8) and I swear by its incredible ability to achieve spectacular flavours. In Egypt, tagines are not widely used, however clay cooking vessels are common, especially in rural villages.

I have been cooking different tagines for my family for many years and this delicious and aromatic seafood tagine is a recent version. Be careful not to overcook the seafood. Serve the tagine as is on the table with buttered couscous.

SERVES 4

1 tablespoon olive oil
1 onion, finely chopped
½ preserved lemon, rind only, rinsed
  and thinly sliced
1 cup (250 ml) water
2 × 160 g ling fillets, skin removed, halved
8 green (raw) king prawns, peeled and
  deveined, tails intact
8 mussels, scrubbed and beards removed
8 scallops off the shell, roe removed
Buttered couscous (see page 152), to serve

CHERMOULA
¼ cup (60 ml) lemon juice, strained
2 tablespoons olive oil
small handful of coriander stems
  and leaves, finely chopped
small handful of flat-leaf parsley,
  leaves picked
1 × 2 cm piece ginger, quartered
2 cloves garlic, peeled and quartered
1 teaspoon salt
1 teaspoon sweet paprika
1 teaspoon ground cumin
4 saffron threads

1 To make the chermoula, place all the ingredients in a food processor and process until well combined, but not a paste. Set aside in a small bowl.

2 Heat the olive oil in a tagine or heavy-based flameproof casserole dish over medium heat and cook the onion for about 2 minutes. Stir in the chermoula and preserved lemon and cook for 2 minutes, until fragrant, then add the water and bring to the boil. Cover and reduce the heat to a gentle simmer for 3 minutes. Add all the seafood and stir to coat with the sauce, then cover again and cook for a further 4–5 minutes. Check that all the mussels have opened, discarding any that have not.

3 Serve immediately with buttered couscous.

POULTRY

POULTRY

Chicken is definitely a once or twice a week meal in my family. There are some delicious, rich chicken dishes in both Korean and Egyptian cuisine.

Poultry features commonly in Korean cooking. One of the most famous Korean dishes is crispy chicken accompanied by a tangy chilli sauce. My mother's version, a slow-braised Korean chicken, is a beloved dish (see page 136) that my family enjoys with hot rice.

Chicken is also popular in Egyptian cuisine, as are game birds such as quails and pigeons. I clearly remember one visit to Alexandria with my family when I was thirteen. My cousin invited me to accompany her to the local markets, with instructions from my grandmother to purchase two chickens for dinner that night. Coming from a Western country, I was oblivious as to what was going to occur at the markets. My cousin purchased two live chickens from a large cage and told me to buy the other requested produce for my grandmother, then to return to pick up the chickens. When I went back they'd been killed and chopped up, so there I was collecting the pieces one by one. Let's just say there was fresh chicken for dinner that night!

I thought I would also include my chicken schnitzel recipe (see page 125), which is neither Korean or Egyptian, but is one of my favourite dishes. It is a recipe I picked up living here in Australia, and have adjusted slightly to make it my own.

Quails stuffed with couscous

SALWAA WA CUSCUS

In Egypt, game birds such as quails and pigeons are widely enjoyed. This spiced couscous filling, sweetened with juicy currants, helps the bird keep its shape while adding depth of flavour.

=== SERVES 4 ===

½ cup (100 g) couscous
½ cup (125 ml) boiling water
1 teaspoon unsalted butter
50 g pine nuts
100 ml olive oil
1 onion, finely chopped
1 clove garlic, finely chopped
50 g currants

2 teaspoons baharat (see page 7)
1 tablespoon finely chopped
   flat-leaf parsley
salt
4 quails, cleaned (ask your butcher
   to do this for you)
1 cup (250 ml) vegetable stock
lemon wedges, to serve

1 Place the couscous in a bowl and pour over the boiling water. Cover tightly with plastic film and leave to steam for 3 minutes. Add the butter and, when it's melted, fluff the couscous with a fork. Set aside.

2 Preheat the oven to 180°C. Spread the pine nuts over a baking tray and toast in the oven for about 5 minutes, until they are golden-brown, shaking the tray occasionally so they don't burn.

3 Heat 1 tablespoon of olive oil in a frying pan over high heat and fry the onion and garlic for 2 minutes, until fragrant. Stir in the currants and toasted pine nuts and cook for a further 2 minutes, then add 1 teaspoon of baharat and the cooked couscous and mix well. Turn off the heat, then add the parsley and season with salt. Set aside to cool.

4 Fill the quail cavities with the couscous mixture. Drizzle 1 tablespoon of olive oil over the stuffed quails and season with salt. Truss the quails' legs.

5 Heat the remaining olive oil in a non-stick frying pan over medium heat, then add the quails and sear all over for about 5 minutes, until the skin begins to turn golden. Add the stock and the remaining baharat. Bring to the boil, then cover with a lid or foil and cook the quails for 10 minutes, turning twice. Remove from the heat and leave to rest for 5 minutes.

6 Serve the stuffed quails with lemon wedges.

Egyptian lemon and garlic chicken

DAJAJ BI LAYMOON WA TOOM

One night, my father told me that he was inviting a friend over for dinner and asked me to make sure there was enough food to include our guest. It was this dish that his friend absolutely loved, saying that he would come back, not to see my father but to eat more of this chicken! It has a wonderful citrus tang, but it is the garlic that really makes the dish so irresistible.

=== SERVES 4 ===

½ cup (125 ml) lemon juice, strained
   (lemon halves reserved)
2 cups (500 ml) chicken stock
10 cloves garlic, peeled and halved
1 teaspoon baharat (see page 7)
salt and freshly ground black pepper

4 chicken marylands
   (leg and thigh portions)
2 tablespoons olive oil
2 potatoes, cut into 1 cm thick slices
1 onion, cut into 1 cm thick slices
handful of flat-leaf parsley,
   leaves roughly chopped

1 Preheat the oven to 180°C.

2 Place the lemon juice, chicken stock, garlic and baharat in a small jug, season to taste with salt and pepper and mix well. Set aside.

3 Using a sharp knife, make three or four deep cuts (down to the bone) in each piece of chicken, to help the flavours infuse.

4 Heat the olive oil in a large frying pan over medium heat. When it is hot, add the chicken pieces, season with ½ teaspoon of salt and ⅓ teaspoon of pepper and cook for about 2–3 minutes on each side, until golden-brown. Remove from the heat.

5 In a baking tin, arrange the potato slices in a single layer, then place the chicken pieces on top. Arrange the onion slices on and around the chicken, then pour the lemon juice mixture over the chicken and vegetables. Add the reserved lemon halves to the tin, then cover it tightly with foil.

6 Bake in the oven for 30 minutes, then remove the foil and gently baste the chicken with the cooking juices. Return to the oven for another 20 minutes.

7 Remove from the oven and garnish with parsley. Serve straight from the baking tin, together with the vegetables and pan juices.

My chicken schnitzel

Who doesn't love a chicken schnitzel, whether it's served in a sanger with fries or on its own with a wedge of lemon and mayonnaise? When I make my schnitzel, I like to add herbs and lemon zest to the batter to give it a more homely flavour. I also use ghee rather than butter for frying, as I find it prevents the coating from browning too quickly, resulting in a crunchy crumb with an even golden colour.

—— SERVES 6 ——

2 eggs
1 teaspoon finely grated lemon zest
2 sprigs marjoram, leaves finely chopped
3 sprigs thyme, leaves finely chopped
salt and freshly ground black pepper
6 × 100 g chicken schnitzel breast fillets

½ cup (75 g) plain flour
1 cup (100 g) packaged breadcrumbs
½ cup (116 g) ghee
6 lemon wedges, to serve

1 In a shallow bowl, combine the eggs, lemon zest, marjoram and thyme with ½ teaspoon of salt and ⅓ teaspoon of pepper.

2 Pat the chicken pieces dry with paper towels. Take a piece of chicken and place it between two sheets of plastic film. Using a meat tenderiser, flatten the chicken until it is roughly 1 cm thick. Set aside and repeat with the rest of the chicken pieces.

3 Season the flour with ½ teaspoon of salt and place it in a shallow bowl. Place the breadcrumbs in another bowl. To crumb the chicken, dip each fillet in the flour, covering it completely and patting off any excess, then dip it in the egg mixture, covering it completely and allowing any excess to drip off. Finally, coat each chicken fillet in breadcrumbs, pressing down firmly on each side. Transfer the crumbed chicken to a clean plate or tray and place in the fridge for 30 minutes to help set the breadcrumbs.

4 Preheat the oven to 150°C.

5 Melt the ghee in a frying pan over medium heat. Place two or three chicken fillets in the frying pan and cook for 3–4 minutes on each side, until golden brown. Remove the cooked schnitzels and keep warm in the oven. Repeat until all the schnitzels are cooked, adding extra ghee, 1 tablespoon at a time, to the pan if necessary.

6 Serve immediately with lemon wedges.

Best chicken soup and risoni

SHORBAT DAJAJ BI USFUR LISAN

In our household, when someone is sick we think the best medicine is honey and lemon tea, and a bowl of chicken soup. For me, there is nothing more comforting than this dish. I have adapted this recipe over time, adding cinnamon and mastic to create an intriguing flavour, and lemon juice at the suggestion of my father and Eman, as they enjoy the zing it adds.

=== SERVES 4 ===

2 tablespoons olive oil
2 chicken carcasses (ask your butcher
   for these)
2 onions, peeled and quartered
2 sticks celery, cut into 2 cm pieces
1 large carrot, peeled and cut into
   2 cm pieces
5 cloves garlic, peeled and quartered
small bunch of flat-leaf parsley, leaves
   roughly chopped and stems reserved

1 cinnamon stick
4 small pieces mastic (see page 7) (optional)
4 bay leaves
3 litres water
salt and freshly ground black pepper
220 g chicken thigh fillets, trimmed of fat
1 cup (220 g) risoni
⅓ cup (80 ml) lemon juice, strained
roughly chopped flat-leaf parsley (extra),
   to garnish

1 Heat the olive oil in a large, heavy-based saucepan over medium–high heat. Add the chicken carcasses and cook, turning frequently, for 5–7 minutes, until browned. Add the onion, celery, carrot and garlic and cook for 5 minutes, until the vegetables begin to soften. Add the parsley stems, cinnamon stick, mastic (if using), bay leaves and water, and bring to the boil. Boil for 2 minutes, then reduce the heat to a gentle simmer and cook, covered, for 2 hours. Every 20 minutes or so, use a slotted spoon to carefully skim off any impurities floating on the surface.

2 Using a fine sieve or a large piece of muslin, strain the chicken soup into a large bowl, then season to taste with salt and pepper. Discard the solids. Return the soup to the saucepan and add the chicken fillets. Simmer gently, covered, over medium heat for 10–12 minutes. Remove the chicken fillets and set aside.

3 Add the risoni and lemon juice, and cook for 10 minutes or until the risoni is tender, giving the soup a good stir every few minutes. While the soup is cooking, shred the chicken into small pieces and divide among four bowls.

4 Ladle the soup over the chicken in the bowls and serve immediately, garnished with the chopped parsley leaves.

Jute leaves soup

MOLOKHIA

Molokhia is the pride and joy of every Egyptian. It is certainly one of my favourite dishes as it gives me such a homely, comforting feeling every time I eat it. My mouth is already watering! Molokhia is a Middle Eastern leafy green vegetable, available fresh from markets or dried and frozen from Middle Eastern grocers. In the Egyptian and Palestinian versions of this dish, the molokhia leaves are finely chopped and the resulting soup is wonderfully thick and starchy. The Lebanese and Syrian versions use the whole leaves and the result is less 'gloopy', but my family members refuse to eat molokhia unless they are able to pick the soup up, leaving behind a starchy trail!

=== SERVES 4 ===

¼ cup (58 g) ghee
1 × 1.4 kg chicken, skin removed
4 onions, peeled and quartered
2 cloves garlic, peeled and halved
2 bay leaves
1 teaspoon ground cumin
1 teaspoon ground coriander
2 litres water

800 g finely chopped frozen molokhia
½ bunch of coriander, leaves and stems
4 cloves garlic (extra), peeled
1 teaspoon tomato paste (puree)
salt and freshly ground black pepper
Rice with vermicelli (see page 81),
 to serve (optional)

1 Heat 1 tablespoon of ghee in a large, heavy-based saucepan or stockpot over medium heat. Add the chicken and cook for about 3–5 minutes, until browned all over. Add the onion and garlic and cook for about 2 minutes, until fragrant. Add the bay leaves, cumin, coriander and water and bring to the boil over high heat. Boil for 2 minutes, then place the lid on the pan, reduce the heat and simmer gently for 1 hour. Using a slotted spoon, carefully skim off any impurities floating on the surface. After 1 hour, use tongs to transfer the chicken to a large plate, then cover with plastic film and set aside.

2 Add the molokhia to the pan, increase the heat to medium and cook for 5 minutes. Reduce the heat and simmer the soup gently for 20 minutes. Stir only once, very gently.

3 Very finely chop the coriander and extra garlic using a food processor. Heat 1 tablespoon of ghee in a frying pan over medium heat and add the chopped coriander and garlic. Cook for about 3 minutes or until fragrant, stirring frequently to prevent the mixture from burning. Add the garlic and coriander mixture to the soup, then stir in the tomato paste and season to taste with salt and pepper, mixing gently and quickly. The soup should be thick, not watery.

4 Using your fingers, break the chicken into small pieces, discarding the bones. Heat the remaining ghee in a frying pan over medium heat, then cook the chicken for about 3–5 minutes, until golden and crispy. Season with salt and pepper to taste.

5 Ladle the soup into bowls. Serve with chicken pieces and, if you like, rice with vermicelli on separate serving plates, and allow everyone to help themselves.

Chicken with lamb and rice

ROZ BI DAJAJ

I love entertaining and this dish is always a winner. Traditionally, you pack the rice mixture tightly into a mould, then carefully unmound it before placing the chicken on top. Here, I have made it all a bit looser. The use of nuts as a garnish is traditional in Middle Eastern cuisine and heightens the overall flavour of the dish, as well as adding a crunchy texture. Present this dish at your next gathering and I promise it will be a hit!

—— SERVES 6 ——

3 cups (600 g) long-grain rice
salt
2 tablespoons olive oil
½ onion, finely chopped
1 clove garlic, crushed
300 g lamb mince
1 teaspoon baharat (see page 7)
½ teaspoon ground cinnamon
1 cup (160 g) blanched almonds, halved
¼ cup (40 g) pine nuts

CHICKEN STOCK

2 tablespoons olive oil
1 × 1.6 kg chicken, skin removed and
    quartered (ask your butcher to do this)
1 onion, peeled and quartered
3 cloves garlic, peeled and halved
5 pieces mastic (see page 7)
2 cinnamon sticks
1 tablespoon baharat
salt and freshly ground black pepper
1.25 litres water

1 Soak the rice in salted water for 30 minutes, then rinse and drain.

2 Meanwhile, to make the chicken stock, heat the olive oil in a large, heavy-based saucepan over medium–high heat. Add the chicken pieces and cook for 3 minutes to brown, then add the onion and garlic and cook for 3 minutes, until fragrant. Add the mastic, cinnamon sticks and baharat and season to taste with salt and pepper. Add the water and bring to the boil over high heat, then reduce the heat to low and simmer gently, covered, for 45 minutes or until the chicken is just tender. Drain the chicken in a colander, reserving the stock in a large bowl. Place the chicken in a bowl and cover tightly with plastic film. Allow the chicken to cool, then strip the meat from the bones, cut into shreds and set aside, covered. Discard the skin and bones.

3 Heat the olive oil in a large, heavy-based saucepan over medium heat and fry the onion and garlic for about 3 minutes, until fragrant. Increase the heat to high, then add the lamb mince, baharat, ground cinnamon and 1 teaspoon of salt and cook, stirring to break up the mince, for 3–4 minutes, until the lamb mince is almost cooked through.

4 Add the drained rice, stirring well until all the grains are thoroughly coated with the lamb mixture. Add 1 litre of the reserved chicken stock and bring to the boil over high heat. Cover tightly with the lid, then reduce to the lowest heat and cook for 25–30 minutes, until the liquid has been absorbed. Remove from the heat and set aside, covered, for 10 minutes. Remove the lid and give the rice a good fluff with a fork, then replace the lid.

5 Toast the almonds and pine nuts separately in a frying pan over medium heat for about 3 minutes, until golden-brown.

6 Place the rice mixture onto a large serving platter, top with the shredded chicken, then scatter with toasted almonds and pine nuts and serve immediately.

Chicken kebabs with garlic yoghurt

SHISH TAWOOK DAJAJ WA ZABADY BI TOOMB

Like every Australian family, my family loves a good barbecue. My mother prefers to barbecue chicken than red meats, and I always make this special marinade. Serve the kebabs with the delicious garlic yoghurt, flatbread and salad . . . that is, if they even reach your plate – they have been known to disappear straight from the barbecue! If you can, start this recipe a day ahead so the chicken can marinate overnight.

=== SERVES 4 ===

600 g chicken thigh fillets, trimmed of fat
   and cut into bite-sized pieces
vegetable oil, for greasing

GARLIC YOGHURT
1 cup (280 g) natural yoghurt
2 cloves garlic, minced
1 tablespoon lemon juice, strained
½ teaspoon salt

MARINADE
¼ cup (60 ml) lemon juice, strained
2 tablespoons olive oil
2 cloves garlic, finely chopped
1 teaspoon salt
1 teaspoon paprika
1 teaspoon finely chopped oregano
1 teaspoon finely chopped flat-leaf parsley
½ teaspoon ground cumin
½ teaspoon ground coriander
½ teaspoon ground fenugreek (available
   from Middle Eastern and Indian grocers)
⅓ teaspoon freshly ground black pepper

1 To make the garlic yoghurt, place all the ingredients in a small bowl and mix well. Cover with plastic film and set aside in the fridge.

2 To make the marinade, combine all the ingredients in a large bowl.

3 Add the chicken to the marinade and massage in with your fingers, so that the chicken pieces are thoroughly coated. Cover with plastic film and marinate in the fridge for at least 6 hours, or overnight.

4 If using bamboo skewers, soak them in ice-cold water for 30 minutes before use to prevent them from scorching on the barbecue. Remove the marinated chicken from the fridge and thread onto the skewers.

5 Preheat the barbecue to medium for about 5 minutes before using. Lightly oil the grill to prevent the chicken from sticking, then cook the kebabs for 3–4 minutes each side, turning twice, until browned and cooked through. You could also use a grill pan, but the chicken is far more flavoursome if you use the barbecue.

6 Serve the kebabs with the garlic yoghurt on the side.

Mum's spicy chicken

DAKJJIM

This is my mother's recipe, which was handed down from her mother, my *halmony* (grandmother). Mum always makes it really spicy – although she assures us all that it is never hot enough. It is the perfect recipe for winter nights, as it is certain to warm you up. I love spooning out the sauce and eating it with rice.

=== SERVES 4 ===

1 kg chicken drumsticks, skins removed
2 onions, peeled and cut into thick wedges
2 carrots, peeled and cut into 2 cm
    thick slices
4 potatoes, peeled and cut into wedges
2 tablespoons Korean cooking glucose
    syrup (available from Korean
    grocery stores)
    or 2 tablespoons sugar
1 cup (250 ml) water
spring onions, trimmed and sliced on the
    diagonal, to garnish
steamed rice, to serve (optional)

MARINADE
1 cup (250 ml) water
½ cup (125 ml) dark soy sauce
¼ cup (60 ml) sesame oil
2 tablespoons coarse kochukaru
    (Korean chilli powder; see page 12)
1 tablespoon minced ginger
3 cloves garlic, minced
2 long red chillies, cut into 1 cm pieces
½ teaspoon freshly ground black pepper

1 To make the marinade, combine all the ingredients in a large, shallow dish.

2 Add the chicken to the marinade and stir to coat thoroughly. Cover with plastic film and marinate in the fridge for 2 hours.

3 Place the chicken and marinade in a large, heavy-based saucepan over high heat and cook for 5 minutes, until the sauce comes to the boil. Stir once, then continue to boil over high heat for 10 minutes. Add the onion, carrot and potato and stir together, then add the glucose syrup or sugar and water. Reduce the heat to a gentle simmer and cook for 45 minutes, giving it a gentle stir (avoid breaking the vegetables) every 10 minutes.

4 Garnish with spring onion and serve hot with steamed rice, if you like.

Chicken tagine with preserved lemon and green olives

TAGIINE BI DAJAJ BI LAYMOON WA ZAITOON

A few years ago in Fes, I was sitting in a beautiful *riad* (Moroccan residence with an interior courtyard), amazed by the architecture, waiting for dinner to be served. Suddenly, a beautiful terracotta tagine arrived at the table, and when the lid was removed the contents were revealed – chicken braised with preserved lemons and green olives. The aroma intoxicated me and that dish inspired this one, which is one of my favourites. I am very lucky – my mother preserves her own lemons from a lemon tree that has been growing in our backyard for over fifteen years. I love to use her preserved lemons in this recipe.

═══ **SERVES 4** ═══

1 tablespoon finely chopped ginger
3 cloves garlic, roughly chopped
¼ cup (60 ml) olive oil
2 tablespoons ras el hanout
1 tablespoon sweet paprika
1 tablespoon ground cumin
small bunch of coriander, stems and leaves
⅓ cup (80 ml) lemon juice, strained
1 teaspoon sea salt

1 kg chicken thigh fillets, trimmed of fat and halved
1 onion, thinly sliced
3 preserved lemons, rind only, rinsed and thinly sliced
1 cup (120 g) green olives, pitted and rinsed
2 cups (500 ml) chicken stock (or water)
Buttered couscous (see page 152), to serve (optional)

1 Place the ginger and garlic in a food processor and process until minced. Add the olive oil, spices, coriander, lemon juice and salt and blitz until the coriander is finely chopped.

2 Transfer the marinade to a tagine (see page 8) or a heavy-based flameproof casserole dish, and add the chicken. Massage the marinade into the chicken pieces with your fingers so that the chicken is thoroughly coated. Cover with plastic film and marinate in the fridge for 1 hour.

3 Remove from the fridge and arrange the onion and preserved lemon and olives on top of the chicken. Gently pour the stock over. Place the tagine over low heat and bring slowly to the boil, gently increasing the heat to high, then boil for 5 minutes. Cover with the lid, then reduce the heat to a gentle simmer and cook for 1 hour, stirring every 15 minutes so the chicken does not stick to the bottom.

4 Remove the tagine from the heat. Serve immediately with buttered couscous, if you like.

Sweet and sour chicken

TANG SU YEOK

Korean cuisine has been influenced by Chinese cooking – this dish has elements of the classic sweet and sour chicken. The main distinction is that this version has a very crunchy batter.

====== SERVES 4 ======

1 cup (100 g) tapioca starch
2 cups (500 ml) water
1 egg white
1 tablespoon cornflour
1 tablespoon soy sauce
1 clove garlic, minced
½ teaspoon freshly ground black pepper
600 g chicken thigh fillets, trimmed of fat
    and cut into 1 cm strips
1 litre vegetable oil, for deep-frying
steamed rice, to serve

SWEET AND SOUR SAUCE
1 tablespoon vegetable oil
1 onion, thinly sliced
6 shiitake mushrooms, sliced into thirds
1 carrot, peeled and thinly sliced

¼ red capsicum (pepper), seeds and
    membrane discarded, sliced on diagonal
¼ green capsicum (pepper), seed and pith
    discarded, sliced on diagonal
1 cucumber, peeled, seeded
    and thinly sliced
1 red chilli, seeded and sliced
    on the diagonal
120 g tinned diced pineapple, in natural
    juices (reserve the juice)
2 tablespoons soy sauce
1 teaspoon salt
½ teaspoon freshly ground black pepper
¼ cup (55 g) caster sugar
½ cup (125 ml) apple cider vinegar
1½ cups (375 ml) water
2 tablespoons cornflour, mixed with
    1 tablespoon water

1 Place the tapioca starch and water in a deep bowl and mix well. Set aside for 3 hours. The water will separate from the starch – carefully discard the water, leaving the thick starch. Gently stir in the egg white and cornflour.

2 Place the soy sauce, garlic and pepper in a large bowl, add the chicken and stir to coat thoroughly. Cover with plastic film and marinate in the fridge for 1 hour.

3 Heat the vegetable oil in a deep heavy-based saucepan or wok until it registers 180°C on a thermometer (or a cube of bread dropped into the oil browns in 20 seconds). Remove the chicken from the fridge and dip it into the batter, a few pieces at a time. Add to the hot oil, in small batches, and deep-fry for 3 minutes, until the pieces rise to the surface and are slightly golden-brown. Remove with a slotted spoon and drain on paper towels.

4 To make the sweet and sour sauce, heat the vegetable oil in a large frying pan over high heat, then add the onion and fry for 1 minute. Add the mushrooms and cook for 2 minutes, then add the carrot, capsicum, cucumber, chilli and pineapple. Add the soy sauce, salt, pepper, sugar, vinegar, water and reserved pineapple juice and bring to the boil. Reduce the heat to medium and add the cornflour paste, stirring to avoid any lumps forming. Cook for 3 minutes, until the sauce has thickened.

5 Reheat the oil in the deep heavy-based saucepan or wok and deep-fry the chicken once more, in batches, until lightly browned and crispy. Remove and drain on paper towels.

6 Arrange the chicken on a serving platter and top with the hot sweet and sour sauce. Serve immediately with hot steamed rice.

Harissa chicken

This recipe is full of vibrant flavours. Cooking the chicken over charcoal results in an amazing smokiness, but it still tastes delicious if you use a barbecue grill. Harissa is a North African spice paste made with roasted capsicum. You are always welcome to add more chilli if you like it hot! You'll need to start this recipe the day before.

=== SERVES 4 ===

4 chicken marylands
   (leg and thigh portions)
1 lemon
flatbread and green salad,
   to serve (optional)

HARISSA PASTE
1 red capsicum (pepper)
¼ cup (60 ml) olive oil
1 red chilli, seeded
2 cloves garlic, peeled
1 × 3 cm piece ginger, peeled
1 tablespoon sweet paprika
1 tablespoon ground cumin
1 teaspoon ground coriander
1 teaspoon salt

1   To make the harissa paste, preheat the grill on high. Place the whole capsicum under the hot grill and cook, turning occasionally, until the skin is almost black. Transfer to a heatproof bowl and cover with plastic wrap, then set aside to cool completely. Once cool, carefully peel away the blackened skin and remove the stalks and seeds. Put the capsicum flesh and the rest of the harissa ingredients in a food processor and blend to a thick paste.

2   Using your fingers, carefully separate the skin on the thigh part of each chicken piece to create a pocket, ensuring that the skin is still attached to the flesh. Gently insert a heaped teaspoon of the harissa paste into the space between the meat and the skin. Rub the rest of the harissa paste all over the chicken pieces, then tightly pack them into a plastic container. Cover and marinate in the fridge overnight.

3   Preheat the charcoals or barbecue to hot. Cook the chicken pieces on one side for 6 minutes, then turn and cook for a further 6 minutes. Using a sharp knife, cut a small wedge right to the bone to ensure that the chicken has cooked all the way through.

4   Remove the cooked chicken pieces from the heat and squeeze lemon juice all over them. Serve hot with flatbread and a green salad, if you like.

Spicy, sticky Korean chicken drumettes

Who doesn't love sticky chicken nibblies? With its rich tang, Korean-style chicken is a growing trend in Australia and this recipe is a great one to try at home. Eat it straight from the oven while hot and be warned that it is fairly spicy, so make sure you have a cold drink nearby! If you can't get drumettes, you can use chicken wings instead. You'll need to start this recipe the day before.

=== SERVES 4 ===

¼ cup (60 ml) soy sauce
¼ cup (60 ml) water
¼ cup (55 g) white sugar
2 tablespoons kochukaru
   (Korean chilli powder; see page 12)
2 cloves garlic, minced
1 tablespoon vegetable oil
1 tablespoon sesame oil
1 tablespoon minced ginger

1 tablespoon gochujang (Korean hot
   pepper paste; see page 12)
1 tablespoon honey
1 tablespoon sesame seeds
1 kg chicken drumettes
3 spring onions, trimmed and finely sliced,
   to garnish
sliced red chilli, to serve

1 Place all the ingredients except the chicken drumettes and spring onions in a large bowl and mix until well combined.

2 Add the chicken drumettes and toss to coat thoroughly in the marinade, then cover with plastic film and marinate in the fridge overnight.

3 Preheat the oven to 200°C. Lightly grease a baking tray and cover it with baking paper.

4 Place the chicken drumettes with their marinade on the prepared tray in a single layer. Cover with foil and bake for 15 minutes. Remove the foil, then turn the chicken drumettes over, spooning the marinade over the top to baste them. Bake for a further 20 minutes, until the sauce becomes sticky and the chicken drumettes are cooked through.

5 Serve hot, garnished with spring onion and sliced chilli on the side.

MEAT

MEAT

I remember going to the butcher as a child and not having a clue what to order. Lucky for me, my mother was there to show me the ropes – how to pick out fresh meat and the right cuts for the dish. Mum's golden rule when selecting meat was to ensure that the butcher removed as much fat as possible, so that the meat did not need to be trimmed any further when it was time to cook it. Even today, she still insists on viewing each piece of meat and occasionally choosing her own cuts to be minced.

In Middle Eastern (and Korean) cooking, meat is generally cooked for a long time, either in a stew with vegetables or in a soup. The concept of leaving the meat 'pink' is unheard of. Egyptians favour veal and lamb in their stews, cooked until very soft and laced with spices, garlic and coriander.

Koreans cook fewer stews, but more soups using beef on the bone, especially cuts such as the tail or marrow. Although you'll find a few stews that use beef braised in a soy-sauce base, soups are more popular. They are incredibly tasty and a favourite with rice and kimchi in the icy Korean winters. Lamb is rarely used in Korean cooking; this explains why most Koreans don't like the aroma of lamb or mutton.

One piece of advice when you are making meat dishes with lengthy cooking times – use gentle heat, and patience is important!

Middle Eastern baked eggs

SHAKSHUKA

Shakshuka is a wonderful mishmash of ingredients, put together to create a delicious baked egg breakfast or brunch dish. When I am at home with my family on the weekend, I cook this dish in a tagine and place it in the centre of the table for everyone to share. It looks spectacular and smells fabulous. All you need is fresh bread and pickles on the side. I have used sujuk here, a spicy cured Turkish sausage. You could also try another Middle Eastern cured meat, basturma, which is often enjoyed with fried eggs for breakfast. Both can be found at most Middle Eastern grocery stores or butchers. If unavailable, use chorizo instead.

=== SERVES 4–6 ===

200 g sujuk, cut into 1 cm thick
   slices on the diagonal
½ onion, finely chopped
1 clove garlic, finely chopped
300 g canned chickpeas, rinsed twice
   and drained
1 × 400 g can diced tomatoes
½ teaspoon sumac
1 teaspoon ground cumin
1 teaspoon sweet paprika

salt
12 pitted black olives, halved
100 g haloumi, cut into 2 cm cubes
1 small bunch spinach, roughly chopped
6 eggs
roughly chopped flat-leaf parsley,
   to garnish
crusty bread or flatbread, and lemon
   cheeks, to serve

1 Place a heavy-based frying pan over medium heat and fry the sujuk for 3 minutes to allow the fat to render. Using a metal spoon, remove the rendered fat, leaving about 1 tablespoon in the pan. Add the onion and garlic and fry for 2 minutes, until fragrant. Add the chickpeas, tomato, sumac, cumin and paprika and season with salt to taste. Cook for about 2 minutes, until the sauce starts to bubble, then reduce to a gentle simmer. Scatter the olives, haloumi and spinach over the top and cook until the spinach begins to wilt.

2 Make six small indentations in the mixture and gently crack an egg into each one. Cover the pan with a lid or foil and cook for 3 minutes or until the eggs are cooked to your liking; this dish works best if you leave the egg yolks runny.

3 Garnish with parsley, then serve straight from the pan with crusty bread or flatbread, and lemon cheeks alongside.

Lamb, prune and fig tagine with buttered couscous

On a recent trip to Morocco, my sister and I experienced a world of flavours. I sampled this tagine in a restaurant in Marrakesh's main square, the Jemaa el-Fna, and was so excited to recreate it for my friends and family when I returned home. I love how Moroccan cuisine harmoniously combines fruit and proteins to sweeten and enhance the flavour of meat. This is especially comforting on cold winter days, served with some buttered couscous alongside . . . yum!

=== SERVES 4 ===

2 tablespoons olive oil
1 onion, finely chopped
2 cloves garlic, crushed
1.2 kg lamb shoulder, trimmed and cut
    into 5 cm cubes (ask your butcher
    to do this for you)
5 cardamom pods
2 cinnamon sticks
4 saffron threads
1 tablespoon ground ginger
1 tablespoon sweet paprika
1 teaspoon ground cumin
1 teaspoon ground turmeric
2 cups (500 ml) vegetable stock

100 g pitted prunes, halved
100 g dried figs, halved
salt
flat-leaf parsley leaves,
    to garnish (optional)

BUTTERED COUSCOUS
1½ cups (300 g) couscous
1 teaspoon salt
½ teaspoon ground cinnamon
½ teaspoon ground cumin
40 g unsalted butter, cut into small pieces
1 cup (250 ml) boiling water

1 Heat the olive oil in a tagine (see page 8) or a large flameproof casserole dish over medium heat. Add the onion and garlic and cook, stirring, for 3 minutes, until fragrant. Increase the heat to high, then add the lamb and sear all over for a few minutes until well browned, stirring regularly. Reduce the heat to medium, then add the cardamom, cinnamon sticks, saffron, ginger, paprika, cumin and turmeric and cook for about 30 seconds, until the spices are fragrant.

2 Add the vegetable stock and bring to the boil, then reduce the heat to a gentle simmer and cook, covered, for 45 minutes, giving the tagine a good stir every 20 minutes or so. Stir in the prunes and figs and cook, covered, for a further 45 minutes. The lamb should be tender and the dried fruit starting to break up. Season the sauce with salt to taste.

3 While the tagine is cooking, make the buttered couscous. Place the couscous, salt, cinnamon and cumin in a bowl and stir in the butter. Pour in the boiling water, mix quickly and immediately cover with plastic film so that the steam is captured. Leave to steam for 5 minutes, then uncover and fluff up the grains with a fork.

4 Garnish the lamb tagine with parsley, if you like, and serve in the tagine or casserole dish with the couscous in a large serving bowl alongside.

Marinated lamb kebabs

SHAWARMA

Everyone knows Greek yeeros (*gyros*) and Turkish doner kebabs, but in the Middle East we have our own version, known as *shawarma*. The lamb is cut into thin strips, marinated with potent spices and fried over high heat – delicious. It is one of many amazing street foods found throughout Egypt and is a must-try when roaming the bustling streets. Serve the lamb with garlicky yoghurt, salad and flatbread in the centre of the table and everyone can make their own wraps. The pickled cucumbers and pink turnip pickles are available from Middle Eastern shops. If you can, start this recipe a day ahead so the meat can marinate overnight.

=== SERVES 4 ===

500 g lamb backstraps, cut into thin strips
1 tablespoon olive oil
small handful of flat-leaf parsley leaves,
    roughly chopped
small handful of mint leaves
½ red onion, cut into thin slices
1 tomato, cut into thin slices
5 pickled Lebanese (short) cucumbers,
    drained and thinly sliced (or gherkins)
½ cup (100 g) Middle Eastern pink turnip
    pickles (or mixed vegetable pickles)
flatbread, to serve

MARINADE
1 onion, roughly chopped
2 cloves garlic, peeled and halved
2 tablespoons olive oil
1 tablespoon white vinegar
1 teaspoon salt
1 tablespoon baharat (see page 7)

GARLICKY YOGHURT
½ cup (140 g) Greek-style yoghurt
1 clove garlic, finely chopped
1 teaspoon extra virgin olive oil
½ teaspoon salt

1 To make the marinade, place all of the ingredients in a food processor and blitz to combine. Transfer to a large bowl and add the lamb strips, massaging the marinade into the lamb so it is thoroughly coated. Cover with plastic film and place in the fridge for at least 2 hours, preferably overnight, to marinate.

2 To make the garlicky yoghurt, place all the ingredients in a small bowl and mix well.

3 Heat the olive oil in a large heavy-based frying pan over high heat and fry the lamb, in two batches, for about 3 minutes, until just cooked, turning regularly. Transfer to a serving platter and cover with foil to keep warm.

4 Place the herbs, onion, tomato and pickled vegetables on a separate platter. Serve alongside the lamb, with the garlicky yoghurt and flatbread also on the table, and allow guests to help themselves. To assemble, place a piece of flatbread on a plate, spoon some lamb down the middle and drizzle with the garlicky yoghurt. Top with herbs, onion, tomato and pickled vegetables. Roll up the sides of the bread and eat.

Slow-braised lamb shanks with baby onions and dates

HAMAL BI BASAL WA TAMR

This hearty stew is another great winter meal for your family. Slow-braising results in lamb that is so succulent, it just falls off the bone. The sweet onions and spices will fill your home with an irresistible aroma, while the deep, rich flavours will warm and comfort you.

=== SERVES 4 ===

2 tablespoons olive oil
4 cloves garlic, finely chopped
4 lamb shanks
16 baby onions, peeled
2 sprigs marjoram
1 tablespoon sweet paprika

1 teaspoon ground coriander
4 tomatoes, roughly chopped
8 medjool dates, pitted and halved
1.5 litres beef stock
salt and freshly ground black pepper
Buttered couscous (see page 152), to serve

1 Preheat the oven to 160°C.

2 Heat the olive oil in a large flameproof casserole dish over medium heat and fry the garlic for 2 minutes, until fragrant. Add the lamb shanks and sear for a few minutes, until browned all over. Add the baby onions, marjoram, paprika, coriander, tomato, dates and stock and stir well. Bring to the boil, stir again and cover with the lid.

3 Place the casserole in the oven and cook for 1 hour 45 minutes, until the lamb is tender and just falling off the bone. Season with salt and pepper to taste.

4 Serve straight out of the oven with buttered couscous.

Middle Eastern meatballs in tomato sauce

KUFTA BI TAMATIM

Recipes for *kufta* – the Middle Eastern version of the classic meatball – vary throughout the region, as different countries use different spices. Once you have tried this dish, it is very hard to stop yourself from making it every week for your family! Make sure you use a slightly fatty cut of lamb, such as lamb shoulder, and ask your butcher to mince it twice.

======= SERVES 4–6 =======

salt and freshly ground black pepper
roughly chopped flat-leaf parsley,
  to garnish
Rice with vermicelli (see page 81),
  to serve (optional)

MEATBALLS
2 tomatoes
1 large onion, quartered
2 cloves garlic, peeled
large handful of flat-leaf parsley,
  leaves picked
1 teaspoon salt
1 kg twice-minced lamb (ask your butcher
  to do this for you)
1 tablespoon baharat (see page 7)
1 teaspoon ground cinnamon
olive oil, for greasing

TOMATO SAUCE
2 tablespoons olive oil
1 onion, thinly sliced
3 cloves garlic, finely chopped
1 × 400 g can diced tomatoes
600 ml vegetable stock
1 tablespoon tomato paste (puree)
1 teaspoon ground cumin
1 teaspoon mild paprika

1 To make the meatballs, halve the tomatoes, then squeeze out the pulp and roughly chop the flesh. Place the tomato flesh, onion, garlic, parsley and salt in a food processor and process until the vegetables are finely chopped. Strain the mixture through a colander or muslin cloth set over a large bowl, reserving both the vegetables and strained juice.

2 In a large bowl, combine the strained vegetables with the lamb, baharat and cinnamon and mix thoroughly with your hands until the mixture is smooth and well combined. Lightly coat your palms with olive oil (so that the meat doesn't stick) and form tablespoons of the meatball mixture into balls – you should have about 20 balls in total. Put them on a plate, cover with plastic film and refrigerate until needed.

3 To make the tomato sauce, heat the olive oil in a shallow saucepan or deep frying pan over high heat and cook the onion and garlic for 3 minutes, until fragrant. Add the remaining ingredients and strained vegetable liquid, and bring to the boil. Boil for 3 minutes, then cover the pan, reduce the heat to a gentle simmer and cook for 10 minutes, stirring once.

4 Carefully lower the meatballs into the tomato sauce. Increase the heat to high and bring the sauce to the boil for 2 minutes. Reduce the heat to a gentle simmer and cook, covered, for 40 minutes, stirring very gently twice during cooking. Season with salt and pepper to taste.

5 Serve garnished with parsley and accompanied by rice with vermicelli, if you like.

Za'atar-crusted lamb cutlets with rocket salad

Za'atar is a spice blend commonly used in the northern parts of the Middle East. The ingredients can vary, but it generally contains sumac, dried thyme, dried oregano and salt. It is often mixed with oil and used as a dip for bread, but it also makes a very tasty marinade and crust for red meats. It is available from Middle Eastern grocery stores and specialty food stores.

SERVES 4

2 tablespoons za'atar
½ teaspoon salt
2 tablespoons olive oil
1 teaspoon lemon juice, strained
12 lamb cutlets, trimmed of fat
lemon wedges, to serve

ROCKET SALAD
2 handfuls of rocket
250 g cherry tomatoes, halved or quartered
¼ red onion, finely sliced
2 tablespoons extra virgin olive oil
¼ cup (60 ml) lemon juice, strained
salt and freshly ground black pepper

1 Combine the za'atar, salt, olive oil and lemon juice in a large bowl and mix well. Add the lamb cutlets and rub the za'atar mixture all over them, then cover with plastic film and place in the fridge for 1 hour to marinate.

2 Meanwhile, make the rocket salad. Place the rocket, cherry tomato and onion in a large bowl. To make the dressing, place the olive oil and lemon juice in a small bowl and whisk to combine, then season to taste with salt and pepper. Set aside.

3 Preheat the grill plate of your barbecue or a char-grill pan on medium–high heat. Grill the cutlets for 3 minutes on each side or until cooked to your liking.

4 Dress the salad and serve immediately with the cutlets, with lemon wedges on the side.

Grilled beef in soy marinade

BULGOGI

Bulgogi is an iconic Korean dish. You can of course go to a Korean barbecue house to eat it if you like, but it is quite easy (and lots of fun) to make, so why not recreate the atmosphere and dish in your own home? In our household, we cook it on a portable gas cooker at the centre of the table and everyone gets stuck in. Perilla is an Asian herb, whose highly aromatic leaves are used for cooking. You can buy it at Korean food stores. If you can, start this recipe a day ahead so the meat can marinate overnight.

=== SERVES 4 ===

1 × 500 g piece beef scotch fillet,
 thinly sliced
2 spring onions, trimmed and
 cut into 5 cm lengths
1 tablespoon vegetable oil
1 small iceberg lettuce, leaves separated
12 perilla leaves
2 long red chillies, finely sliced
gochujang (Korean hot pepper paste;
 see page 12), to serve
steamed rice and kimchi, to serve (optional)

MARINADE
1 nashi pear, peeled and finely grated
1 onion, halved and thinly sliced
⅓ cup (80 ml) dark soy sauce
¼ cup (60 ml) water
¼ cup (55 g) caster sugar
2 tablespoons sesame oil
3 cloves garlic, minced
1 tablespoon sesame seeds
1 teaspoon minced ginger
½ teaspoon freshly ground black pepper

1 To make the marinade, place all the ingredients in a large bowl and mix to combine.

2 Add the thinly sliced meat and spring onion to the marinade and mix gently. Cover with plastic film and marinate in the fridge for at least 6 hours or overnight.

3 Lightly coat a grill pan with the vegetable oil and place over high heat. Using tongs, divide the beef into two batches and tap to remove any excess marinade. Cook quickly, about 2 minutes per batch, until seared all over.

4 Serve the beef immediately, accompanied by the lettuce, perilla leaves, chilli and gochujang, with steamed rice and kimchi on the side, if you like.

5 Alternatively, if using a portable gas stove, place the oiled grill pan over high heat and place the beef on the table with all the prepared vegetables, gochujang sauce, steamed rice and kimchi. Cook at the table and allow everyone to help themselves to the freshly grilled meat.

Bulgogi sliders with kimchi mayonnaise

Kimchi mayonnaise? Bulgogi sliders? While you might not be convinced of these culinary combinations at first, I promise just one taste of these delectable sandwiches will change your mind! You can get the mini sweet burger buns from Asian bakeries.

=== SERVES 4 ===

vegetable oil, for brushing
8 mini sweet burger buns
¼ small white cabbage, finely shredded
1 nashi pear, peeled, cored and finely sliced (do this just before serving so that the pear doesn't go brown)
1 red onion, finely sliced

KIMCHI MAYONNAISE
1 tablespoon sesame seeds
⅓ cup (100 g) whole egg mayonnaise
¼ cup Baechu kimchi (see page 71), liquid strained and very finely chopped
½ teaspoon salt
1 teaspoon caster sugar

BULGOGI PATTIES
600 g good-quality beef mince
2 spring onions, trimmed and finely sliced
2 cloves garlic, finely chopped
2 tablespoons dark soy sauce
2 tablespoons vegetable oil
1 tablespoon minced ginger
1 egg yolk
1 teaspoon sesame oil
½ teaspoon caster sugar
½ teaspoon salt

1 To make the kimchi mayonnaise, toast the sesame seeds in a dry frying pan over medium heat for about 3 minutes, until golden and fragrant. Combine the sesame seeds with all the other ingredients in a small bowl, then cover with plastic film and place in the fridge until ready to serve.

2 To make the bulgogi patties, place all the ingredients in a large bowl and mix together well. Mould into 8 patties, roughly 1.5 cm high and a bit larger in circumference than the buns, as the meat will shrink when cooked. Place in the fridge for 30 minutes to rest.

3 Heat a char-grill pan over medium heat and lightly brush with vegetable oil. Cook the patties, in two batches, for 3–5 minutes on each side, until cooked through.

4 To assemble, place the bottoms of the buns on serving plates, spoon some kimchi mayonnaise on top, then top with a bulgogi patty, some shredded cabbage, nashi pear and red onion. Finish with the bun top, press lightly and serve immediately.

Peas braised with meat

BAZILLA WA LAHMA

This is my father's favourite stew. When Mum makes a large pot, Dad is content eating it day and night – he never tires of it! The peas and carrot bring a lovely sweetness to the rich beef. You can always omit the meat to create a vegetarian option – boost it with some extra vegetables if you like.

=== SERVES 4 ===

2 tablespoons extra virgin olive oil
1 onion, finely chopped
2 cloves garlic, crushed
400 g gravy beef, cut into 2 cm cubes
500 g peas (fresh or frozen)
1 carrot, peeled and cut into 1 cm cubes

1 teaspoon baharat (see page 71)
3 tomatoes, roughly chopped
3 cups (750 ml) vegetable stock
1 tablespoon tomato paste (puree)
salt and freshly ground pepper
steamed rice, to serve

1 Heat the olive oil in a heavy-based saucepan over high heat and cook the onion and garlic for 3 minutes, until fragrant.

2 Add the beef and sear all over for a few minutes, until well browned.

3 Add the peas, carrot, baharat, tomato, stock and tomato paste, then bring to the boil and boil for 5 minutes.

4 Reduce the heat to a gentle simmer and cook, covered, for 1 hour, until the meat is tender, stirring a couple of times during cooking to prevent anything sticking to the base of the saucepan.

5 Season to taste with salt and pepper, and serve with steamed rice.

Okra and beef stew

BAMIA

This is my Tayta's recipe, which was passed on to my father and in turn to me. It is now one of my favourites. Okra is such an intriguing vegetable, with its unique texture and its wonderful way of soaking up flavour. It is used a lot in Middle Eastern cooking, especially in soups and stews. In Egyptian cooking, taklia (usually garlic and fresh coriander fried in butter or ghee) is used to add an extra burst of flavour to a dish.

=== SERVES 4 ===

500 g small okra
2 tablespoons olive oil
1 onion, finely chopped
500 g topside beef, cut into 3 cm cubes
500 g ripe tomatoes, roughly chopped
2 cups (500 ml) vegetable stock
1 tablespoon tomato paste (puree)
1 teaspoon baharat (see page 7)
1 teaspoon salt
½ teaspoon freshly ground black pepper
2 tablespoons lemon juice, strained
steamed rice, to serve (optional)

TAKLIA
small handful of coriander, stems
    and leaves roughly chopped,
    roots removed
4 cloves garlic, peeled
40 g unsalted butter or ghee
1 teaspoon olive oil

1 Trim the tops and tails of the okra, making sure you maintain their shape. Be careful not to cut them open to expose the inside, as this will release excess starch into the sauce as it cooks. Wash and drain.

2 Heat the olive oil in a large flameproof casserole dish over medium heat. Add the onion and cook for 3 minutes, stirring frequently, until it begins to soften. Add the beef and sear all over for a few minutes, until well browned. Add the tomato, stock, tomato paste, baharat, salt, pepper and lemon juice and bring to the boil. Boil for 2 minutes, then reduce the heat to a gentle simmer and cook, covered, for 45 minutes.

3 Meanwhile, to make the taklia, place the coriander and garlic in a food processor and process until finely chopped. Melt the butter or ghee and the olive oil in a small frying pan over medium heat. Add the coriander and garlic and fry for about 5 minutes, stirring frequently, until the garlic has started to turn golden. Remove from the heat.

4 Add the okra and the taklia to the casserole dish and mix gently. Cook, covered, for a further 30 minutes, until the beef and okra are tender. Serve with steamed rice, if you like.

Beef spare rib soup

GALBI TANG

My mother makes this soup with so much love and attention. She ensures that the stock is rich and flavoursome, and is meticulous about skimming the top so that the broth remains clear. It is always quite a sight to see my sister Eman and my father happily slurping it down and devouring the ribs as quickly as they can! The slippery dang myun noodles, which soak up the hot broth, are another winning component. Don't forget to add a dash of yang nyum jang dressing to add even more flavour to the dish.

===== SERVES 4 =====

1 kg beef spare ribs, cut roughly into
    8 cm × 8 cm pieces, with bones in
    (ask your butcher to do this for you)
salt and freshly ground black pepper
1.5 litres water
4 spring onions, roots intact, washed
    and cut into thirds
4 cloves garlic, peeled and halved

1 × 2.5 cm piece ginger, finely chopped
400 g daikon, peeled and cut into
    2 cm cubes
200 g dang myun noodles (see page 11)
thinly sliced spring onion (extra),
    to garnish
Yang nyum jang dressing (see page 38),
    to serve

1 Soak the beef ribs in a large bowl of cold water with 1 tablespoon of salt for 1 hour. Drain and rinse the ribs a few times, then place in a heavy-based stockpot or large flameproof casserole dish with enough water to cover. Bring to the boil and boil rapidly for 3 minutes, then rinse and drain the ribs. This will help remove any impurities.

2 Return the beef ribs to the pot with the 1.5 litres of water, spring onion, garlic and ginger. Bring to the boil over high heat, then cover with the lid, reduce the heat to a gentle simmer and cook for 1 hour. Remove the lid and use a spoon to skim off any grit, impurities and oil that have risen to the surface, trying not to remove much broth. Add the daikon and cook, covered, for 20 minutes. By this point the meat should be very tender, but still on the bone.

3 About 10 minutes before the soup is ready, bring a large saucepan of water to the boil. Add the noodles and stir immediately to avoid clumping. Boil for about 5 minutes, until the noodles are al dente. Rinse several times in cold water, then leave to drain in a colander.

4 Using a slotted spoon, remove the garlic and spring onion from the soup, then season to taste with salt and pepper.

5 To serve, divide the noodles among four bowls and top with the hot spare ribs and soup. Garnish with extra spring onion and a teaspoon of yang nyum jang dressing.

Beef spare ribs braised with sweet soy sauce

GALBIJIM

I love many things about this dish: the incredibly tender meat that easily falls off the bone, the meaty texture of the black fungus, the subtle heat of the dried chillies and the delicious sweet soy sauce braise.

—— SERVES 4 ——

1 kg beef short spare ribs, trimmed of fat
1 tablespoon salt
1 onion, roughly chopped
12 pieces dried black fungus (see page 11), soaked for 30 minutes
5 dried red chillies, soaked for 30 minutes
steamed rice, to serve (optional)

SWEET SOY SAUCE
3 cups (750 ml) water
½ cup (125 ml) soy sauce
¼ cup (55 g) white sugar
½ teaspoon freshly ground black pepper
5 cloves garlic, minced
1 tablespoon minced ginger
2 tablespoons sesame oil
salt

1 Put the water and salt in a large bowl, add the beef ribs and leave to soak for 1 hour. Drain and rinse the ribs a few times, then place in a heavy-based stockpot or large flameproof casserole dish with enough water to cover. Bring to the boil and boil rapidly for 3 minutes, then rinse and drain the ribs. This will help remove any impurities.

2 To make the sweet soy sauce, combine all the ingredients in a small bowl.

3 Return the ribs to the pot and add the sweet soy sauce, stirring well to make sure the ribs are thoroughly coated. Leave the ribs to marinate for 30 minutes at room temperature.

4 Bring the ribs and sauce to the boil over high heat. Boil for 5 minutes, then reduce the heat to a gentle simmer and cook, covered, for 1 hour 30 minutes.

5 Add the onion and drained black fungus and chillies, then give the whole mixture a good stir. Cook, uncovered, for a further 30 minutes, until the sauce has reduced and the meat is tender. Stir carefully every 10 minutes or so to prevent the ribs from sticking to the base of the pot. Serve hot with steamed rice, if you like.

DESSERTS

- 6 -

DESSERTS

ho doesn't have a love of desserts? A great dessert certainly finishes off the meal successfully, so that all you have left (hopefully) is a group of very happy diners. Dessert can also be a course in itself, accompanied by some rich coffee or exotic tea.

I love desserts that have interesting textures and are not overbearingly sweet. My mother has never been too keen on cooking desserts, although she would create traditional Middle Eastern biscuits like *Maamoul* (see page 179) for celebrations. My father, on the other hand, used to purchase packet chocolate cakes and whip up some crazy blend of nuts and dried fruit to add to the cake mix – they would often turn out to be quite delectable, but sadly he has not done that in a long time now.

There is only a small selection of desserts in Korean cuisine, and they tend to be light, not too rich or sweet. I have included here the recipe for *Hod-dok*, or stuffed sweet fried cakes, which are basically made from dough stuffed with nuts and brown sugar (see page 193) and are very popular as street food.

Middle Eastern sweets, on the other hand, are sweet, rich and have a combination of buttery textures that make them quite unique. Egyptian sweets are much the same as other Middle Eastern sweets, though there are some slight variations.

Whether or not you have a sweet tooth like me, I hope you enjoy this chapter, with its delectable mix of traditional and modern desserts to tantalise your palate.

Stuffed pancakes

ATAYEF

Sweets are made generously during the fasting month of Ramadan. These crispy pancakes stuffed with nuts or qashta, a type of clotted cream, are very popular. They are best eaten warm, and be warned, they are fabulously addictive! Make sure you cook only one side of the pancakes so that they seal properly.

=== MAKES 12–14 ===

vegetable oil, for oiling and deep-frying

ROSEWATER SYRUP
1 cup (220 g) white sugar
⅓ cup (80 ml) water
1 tablespoon rosewater
1 tablespoon lemon juice, strained

PANCAKES
1¼ cups (185 g) plain flour
½ teaspoon dried yeast
½ teaspoon baking powder
1 cup (250 ml) milk
½ cup (125 ml) water

NUT FILLING
⅓ cup (45 g) shelled pistachios, finely chopped
⅓ cup (35 g) walnuts, finely chopped
⅓ cup (45 g) skinned hazelnuts, finely chopped
1½ tablespoons white sugar
1 tablespoon rosewater
1 teaspoon ground cinnamon

1 To make the rosewater syrup, combine the sugar and water in a small saucepan and bring to the boil over high heat, stirring to dissolve the sugar. Reduce the heat to a gentle simmer and cook for 10 minutes, then add the rosewater and lemon juice and simmer for another 2 minutes. Remove from the heat and cool to room temperature.

2 To make the pancakes, place all the ingredients in a bowl and mix with electric beaters or a whisk until well combined. Set aside for 10 minutes at room temperature.

3 To make the nut filling, combine all the ingredients in a small bowl.

4 Lightly grease a large, non-stick frying pan with oil and place over medium heat. Once hot, add about ¼ cup of batter, tapping the pan slightly so that it spreads to about 14 cm in diameter. Cook for 1–1½ minutes, until golden-brown underneath and almost set but light in colour on top. You only need to cook the pancake on one side, so do not flip it. Wait until the batter bubbles, then remove each pancake from the pan and allow to cool on a plate. Continue with the remaining batter to make 12–14 pancakes in total.

5 Place 1 tablespoon of nut filling in the centre of the uncooked side of a pancake. Fold the pancake in half, into a half-moon shape, sealing the edges by pressing them tightly.

6 Heat about 3 cups (750 ml) of vegetable oil in a deep saucepan over high heat. Working in batches, gently lower the filled pancakes into the hot oil and deep-fry for 3–4 minutes, until they are crisp and golden-brown all over. Remove the pancakes with a slotted spoon and place them gently on paper towels to drain briefly, then quickly dip them in the cooled rosewater syrup, draining off any excess. Serve warm on a platter.

CLOCKWISE FROM LEFT:
BISCUITS FILLED WITH DATES OR PISTACHIOS P 179
FRESH MOROCCAN MINT TEA P 180

Biscuits filled with dates or pistachios

MAAMOUL

Maamoul is perhaps the most famous of Middle Eastern biscuits, especially popular for religious celebrations such as Eid and Christmas. You can be as creative as you like with the filling, as long as you create a tight seal to enclose it. You can buy a maamoul mould online or at a Middle Eastern grocery. Otherwise, the prongs of a small fork can help create patterns on top. The grooves will help the icing sugar stick to the biscuit.

=== MAKES ABOUT 40 ===

2 cups (320 g) coarse semolina
1 cup (150 g) plain flour
1 tablespoon caster sugar
1½ teaspoons baking powder
250 g unsalted butter, softened
¼ cup (60 ml) milk
1 tablespoon orange blossom water
vegetable oil, for oiling
1 cup (160 g) pure icing sugar

PISTACHIO FILLING
1 cup (140 g) raw shelled pistachios
1 tablespoon orange blossom water
1½ tablespoons caster sugar

DATE FILLING
1 cup (170g) pitted medjool dates,
  roughly chopped
1 tablespoon orange juice, strained
1 tablespoon orange blossom water

1 Combine the semolina, flour, sugar and baking powder in a large bowl and make a well in the centre. Add the butter, milk and orange blossom water and, using your hands, combine the mixture until it forms a soft, malleable dough. If the mixture is too dry, add a little more milk, and if it is too wet, add a little more plain flour. Cover with plastic film and leave to rest at room temperature for 1 hour.

2 To make the pistachio filling, place all the ingredients in a food processor and process until fine and crumbly. Do not let it reach a paste-like consistency. Transfer to a bowl and clean the food processor.

3 To make the date filling, place all the ingredients in a food processor and process until they form a smooth paste.

4 Preheat the oven to 160°C and line two baking trays with baking paper.

5 Shape a tablespoon of dough into a ball, then gently flatten it in the palm of your hand to make a 6 cm circle. Place 1 teaspoon of either the pistachio or date filling in the centre of the dough, then pinch the edges together so that the filling is completely enclosed and roll into a ball.

6 Lightly oil a maamoul mould with vegetable oil. Press the dough ball firmly into the mould, then tap the mould to remove the patterned biscuit. (If you don't have a maamoul mould, use fork prongs to make patterns.) Repeat to make about 40 biscuits.

7 Place the biscuits on the prepared trays with a 2 cm gap between each. Bake in the oven for 25–30 minutes or until light golden. Transfer the biscuits to wire racks to cool.

8 Place the icing sugar in a bowl. Roll as many cooled biscuits as you'd like to serve in the icing sugar, tapping to remove any excess. Any leftover biscuits can be kept in an airtight container for up to one month – roll in icing sugar just before serving.

Fresh Moroccan mint tea

SHAY BI NA'NA

As a family we always finish a fabulous meal with a pot of tea, as it is the best way to cleanse and refresh the body. Mint tea is one of my absolute favourites. On my recent travels to Morocco, I was often tempted by the fragrance of freshly brewed mint tea, whether in the street, at the markets, or in a restaurant. I like it best served slightly sweet to offset the intense flavour of the fresh mint. *Pictured page 178.*

=========== MAKES 600 ML ===========

2 tablespoons loose green tea leaves
½ bunch mint, leaves picked

about 600 ml boiling water
sugar, to taste

1 Place the green tea leaves and mint in a teapot and add just enough boiling water to cover. Let it stand for 1 minute, then discard the water, keeping the tea and mint in the teapot. Add the 600 ml of boiling water and let the tea infuse for 3–5 minutes, according to your preferred strength.

2 Pour into small tea cups and serve with sugar on the side.

Kataifi pastry with milk custard

KUNAFA

In Egyptian cuisine, *kunafa* refers to kataifi pastry baked with either a milk custard or a nut filling. It is also known as *kunafa sha'riya* or 'hair pastry', because its fine threads of golden pastry resemble hair strands. I prefer the milk custard filling as it is perfectly balanced with the crunchy pastry. The art of making kataifi pastry is fascinating to watch. The batter is released in a rain-like technique over a constantly turning heated brass or copper disc that cooks the pastry instantly.

=== MAKES ABOUT 12 PIECES ===

375 g kataifi pastry (available from
    Middle Eastern and Greek grocers)
1 cup (250 ml) melted ghee, cooled to
    room temperature
1 teaspoon finely grated lemon zest

ORANGE BLOSSOM SYRUP
2 cups (440 g) caster sugar
1½ cups (375 ml) water
1 tablespoon orange blossom water

FILLING
400 ml full-cream milk
600 ml pure cream
1 tablespoon sugar
2 vanilla pods, split lengthways
    and seeds scraped
¼ cup (35 g) cornflour, mixed
    with ¼ cup (60 ml) milk

1   To make the orange blossom syrup, bring the sugar and water to the boil in a saucepan, then reduce the heat and simmer gently for 10 minutes, stirring occasionally to help dissolve all the sugar. Add the orange blossom water and continue to simmer for 2 minutes. Remove from the heat and leave to cool to room temperature.

2   Allow the kataifi pastry to come to room temperature so that it is more malleable. Pour the ghee over the pastry and, using your hands, massage the ghee through all the strands so that they are all golden in colour. Divide the pastry in half.

3   To make the filling, place the milk, cream, sugar and vanilla seeds in a saucepan and bring to the boil. Reduce the heat to medium and slowly add the cornflour paste, mixing with a whisk as you go. Continue to whisk for 3–5 minutes, until the mixture becomes a very thick custard. Remove from the heat and leave to cool slightly.

4   Place half of the kataifi pastry in a 35 cm × 20 cm slice tin, making sure it completely and evenly covers the bottom of the tin. Pour the filling over the pastry, then leave it to rest and thicken for 15 minutes.

5   Preheat the oven to 170°C.

6   Carefully scatter the remaining kataifi pastry over the filling and press down gently. Using an oiled sharp knife, cut the *kunafa* into large squares.

7   Bake for 40 minutes, until the pastry is golden and crunchy. Remove from the oven and carefully spoon over enough syrup to soak through the top layer of kataifi pastry.

8   Serve warm.

Semolina slice with coconut

BASBOUSA BI GOZ EL HIND

This deliciously chewy, syrupy slice was my father's favourite sweet as a boy. He used to buy a few pieces at a time from the local sweet vendors and then eat them all, one after another! Like my father, I enjoy the crunchy yet chewy edges that ooze with syrup. Using both coarse and fine semolina together with desiccated coconut provides an interesting combination of textures.

=== MAKES ABOUT 24 ===

1½ cups (240 g) coarse semolina
1 cup (160 g) fine semolina
¾ cup (165 g) white sugar
½ cup (75 g) self-raising flour
1 cup (80 g) desiccated coconut
220 g unsalted butter, melted and cooled
200 g Greek-style yoghurt
½ cup (80 g) whole blanched almonds
vegetable oil, for greasing

ROSEWATER SYRUP
2 cups (440 g) caster sugar
1½ cups (375 ml) water
1 tablespoon rosewater

1 To make the rosewater syrup, bring the sugar and water to the boil in a saucepan. Reduce the heat and simmer gently for 10 minutes, stirring occasionally to help dissolve all the sugar. Add the rosewater and continue to simmer for 2 minutes. Remove from the heat and leave to cool to room temperature.

2 Place the coarse and fine semolina, sugar, flour and coconut in a bowl and make a well in the centre. Pour the cooled melted butter into the well and add the yoghurt. Combine the ingredients with a spatula, then use your hands to massage the dough until it is soft and comes together.

3 Lightly oil a 35 cm × 20 cm slice tin with vegetable oil. Place the semolina mixture in the tin and spread it out with your hands – it should be about 2 cm deep. Place the tray in the fridge for 15 minutes.

4 Preheat the oven to 180°C.

5 Remove the tin from the fridge. Using an oiled knife, cut the slice on the diagonal into pieces about 3 cm square. Gently press an almond into the centre of each piece.

6 Bake for 40 minutes, until the surface is golden-brown and crusty around the edges, then remove from the oven and pour the cooled syrup evenly over the slice. Allow the slice to cool to room temperature in the tin, then cut into the marked pieces and serve.

Rose petal fruit salad

SALATAH FAWAKIH WA WARDAH

The Australian summer can be quite harsh, and I find that in the midst of the heat there is nothing more refreshing than a chilled fruit salad. We are very blessed to have some of the most amazing produce grown locally and this fruit salad is a wonderful opportunity to show off the stunning flavours and colours of home. The rose petals, with their delicate perfume and beautiful splash of colour, are a lovely finishing touch.

=========== SERVES 4–6 ===========

200 g seedless watermelon, rind removed, cut into 2 cm cubes

200 g honeydew melon, rind removed, cut into 2 cm cubes

200 g rockmelon, rind removed, cut into 2 cm cubes

250 g strawberries, halved

4 ripe figs, quartered

seeds from ½ pomegranate (optional)

3 sprigs mint, leaves picked and torn

2 tablespoons edible rose petals, fresh or dried

1 tablespoon rosewater, or to taste

ice-cream or whipped cream, to serve (optional)

1 Combine all the fruit in a large bowl or on a platter. Scatter over the mint, rose petals and rosewater and toss gently. Cover with plastic film and leave to chill in the fridge for an hour.

2 Gently mix the fruit once more. Serve by itself or with ice-cream or whipped cream.

Braised quince with toasted walnut cream

SAFARJAL BI QASHTA WA JOOZ

Quinces are fascinating fruits, with a lovely delicate tartness. They are a little underused here in Australia, but when in season they are readily available, so I urge you to try them. They change colour as soon as they are cut open or peeled, so it is important to have acidulated water at the ready to protect the fruit from discolouration.

=== SERVES 4 ===

2 cups (500 ml) water
¾ cup (165 g) caster sugar
½ cup (125 ml) verjuice
2 cinnamon sticks
4 cloves
3 star anise
2 large quinces
squeeze of lemon juice
chopped toasted walnuts (extra),
    to serve

TOASTED WALNUT CREAM
¼ cup (25 g) toasted walnuts
¾ cup (180 ml) clotted cream
    (or double cream, lightly whipped)

1 To make the walnut cream, blitz the walnuts in a food processor until finely chopped (but not ground). Gently mix the walnuts through the clotted cream. Cover with plastic film and keep in the fridge until needed.

2 Place the water, sugar, verjuice and spices in a saucepan and mix well. Set aside.

3 Peel the skin off the quinces. Quarter the fruit and remove the hardened inside lining and seeds, then trim the tops and bottoms. Place the quince in cool water with a squeeze of lemon juice (this is called 'acidulated water') to avoid discolouration.

4 Strain the quince pieces and place in the verjuice mixture. Cover and bring to the boil, then reduce the heat to a gentle simmer and braise for 40 minutes. Carefully remove the quince pieces from the sauce, then place in a bowl and cover with plastic film to keep warm and retain moisture. Bring the braising liquid to the boil over medium heat and cook for 10 minutes or until the liquid has reduced to a thick syrup.

5 To serve, arrange some of the quince pieces in a bowl and top with a generous spoonful of the walnut cream. Drizzle over some of the reduced syrup, scatter with extra toasted walnuts and serve warm.

Rice pudding with rosewater

ROZ BI LABAN

This is my absolute favourite dessert. I don't think there is anything more comforting than curling up on the couch indulging in warm rice pudding fragranced with rosewater. The cinnamon and pistachio topping provides a lovely contrast to the soft, creamy rice. This is best served warm – that's if you can resist eating it straight from the pan!

——— SERVES 4–6 ———

¾ cup (150 g) arborio rice
2 cups (500 ml) water
1 litre full-cream milk
¾ cup (165 g) caster sugar

2 tablespoons double cream
1 tablespoon rosewater
⅓ cup (45 g) raw shelled pistachios
1 teaspoon ground cinnamon

1 Bring the rice and water to the boil in a heavy-based saucepan. Add the milk and allow it to return to the boil, then reduce the heat to a gentle simmer and cook for 1 hour 30 minutes, stirring frequently. Add the sugar, cream and rosewater and cook for a further 10 minutes, until the rice is tender, then remove from the heat.

2 In a food processor, blitz the pistachios and cinnamon until well combined and the nuts are finely chopped (but not a paste).

3 Serve the rice pudding warm, sprinkled with a generous amount of the cinnamon and pistachio topping.

Stuffed sweet fried cakes

HOD-DOK

These are sold as street food all over Korea, especially in winter. The dough is toasty and crunchy with just a slight chew, and encases a warm, oozy filling of sugar and nuts. Imagine yourself in a crowded market in Korea in the middle of winter, dressed in your warmest coat and getting cosy with this sweet delight in your hands. How wonderful!

—— MAKES 10 ——

150 ml vegetable oil, plus extra for oiling
plain flour, for kneading and rolling

DOUGH
1 cup (250 ml) lukewarm water
1 tablespoon vegetable oil
1 tablespoon white sugar
2 teaspoons instant dried yeast
2¼ cups (335 g) plain flour

FILLING
⅓ cup (75 g) firmly packed brown sugar
1 teaspoon ground cinnamon
1 tablespoon roasted unsalted peanuts, finely chopped
1 tablespoon walnuts, finely chopped

1 To make the dough, place the water, vegetable oil, sugar and yeast in a large bowl and mix well. Leave to stand for 15 minutes, then add the flour and mix together well. Roll the dough into a ball and place it in a large, oiled bowl. Cover the bowl tightly with plastic film and rest at room temperature for 1 hour, until doubled in size.

2 Tip the dough onto a well-floured surface and knead a few times with floured hands, then return it to the bowl. Leave it to rest, tightly covered with plastic film, for a further 15 minutes.

3 To make the filling, combine all the ingredients in a small bowl and set aside.

4 Tip the dough onto a floured surface and, using floured hands, knead well for 2 minutes, then divide into 10 balls. Place the dough balls on two large plates and cover with plastic film while you work with one dough ball at a time. Using a floured rolling pin, roll the ball out to a disc, about 12 cm in diameter. Place a heaped teaspoon of filling in the centre, then seal the edges and roll into a ball. Gently flatten the ball, ensuring that the dough is sealed, then gently roll it out to a 12 cm disc again and set aside. Repeat the process with the remaining dough and filling.

5 Add enough vegetable oil to a large, heavy-based non-stick frying pan to generously coat the base. Heat over medium heat until hot. Fry the stuffed cakes, in batches, for 1–2 minutes each side, until golden and slightly crunchy. Remove the cakes from the pan with a slotted spoon and drain on paper towels. Wipe the pan clean with a paper towel in between batches and add more vegetable oil. Serve hot.

Halva and fig rounds

Figs are used in both savoury and sweet dishes in the Middle East. I prefer the black figs when they are ripe because of their incredible colours: the black skin with flecks of green and the pulp with its bursts of fuchsia and cream. The taste and texture of the fruit is just amazing. Halva (sweetened and hardened tahini paste) comes plain or with a selection of nuts, and is a must-have pantry item in every Middle Eastern home. The fresh figs mellow out the sweetness of the halva and the combination of textures in this simple dish is divine.

=========== SERVES 4 ===========

2 sheets ready-rolled puff pastry, thawed
⅓ cup (80 g) crumbled halva
4 ripe figs, quartered

1 egg yolk, mixed with 1 tablespoon milk
1 teaspoon white sesame seeds
creme fraiche, to serve

1 Preheat the oven to 180°C and line a baking tray with baking paper.

2 Using a round 12 cm fluted cutter, cut out 8 rounds of puff pastry. Place 1 heaped teaspoon of the crumbled halva in the centre of a pastry round. Arrange a quartered fig in a tight stack on top of the crumbled halva.

3 Place another round of pastry on top of the fig, sealing it tightly to the bottom round of pastry by pressing the edges together. Repeat the process until all four pastry rounds are complete.

4 Brush the tops of the pastries with egg wash, then sprinkle with sesame seeds. Bake in the oven for 20 minutes, until the pastry is golden and crispy.

5 Serve warm with a dollop of creme fraiche.

Middle Eastern suppliers

NEW SOUTH WALES

ABU SALIM SUPERMARKET
151 Waterloo Road
Greenacre NSW 2190
(02) 9740 4600

**BANKSTOWN LEBANESE BAKERY
& MIXED BUSINESS**
287 Chapel Road
Bankstown NSW 2200
(02) 9708 3976

FIVE STARS COFFEE AND NUT ROASTER
85–87 Yerrick Road
Lakemba NSW 2195
(02) 9759 1895

GIMA SUPERMARKET
31–35 Queen Street
Auburn NSW 2144
(02) 9749 4588

HARKOLA FOOD WHOLESALER
3–7 Highgate Street
Auburn NSW 2144
(02) 9737 5888

OTHER STATES

CEDARS OF LEBANON
Shop 4, Building 9
Southlands Centre
Mawson Place
Mawson ACT 2607
(02) 6290 2344

THE ARABIAN GROCER
1941 Logan Road
Upper Mount Gravatt
Brisbane QLD 4122
(07) 3219 4204

ADELAIDE LEBANESE BAKERY
7 Ann Street
Thebarton SA 5031
(08) 8234 9545

A1 MIDDLE EAST FOOD STORE
643–645 Sydney Road
Brunswick VIC 3056
(03) 9386 0440

BASFOODS DIRECT
419 Victoria Street
Brunswick VIC 3056
(03) 9381 1444

OASIS BAKERY
9/993 North Road
Murrumbeena VIC 3163
(03) 9570 1122

AL-WAFA
Shop 29/70 Langford Ave.
Langford WA 6147
(08) 9356 9555

Korean suppliers

NEW SOUTH WALES

HAN YANG GROCERIES
28 The Boulevarde
Strathfield NSW 2135
(02) 9744 9677

HANA ASIAN GROCERY
27 Railway Parade
Eastwood NSW 2122
(02) 9874 1581

HANARO MART
Shop 16/11 The Boulevarde
Strathfield NSW 2135
(02) 9746 5200

KOMART
Shop 5/24 George Street
North Strathfield NSW 2137
(02) 9764 1199

SMILE KOREA MART
636 George Street
Sydney NSW 2000
(02) 9264 4522

WOORI GROCERY
357 Burwood Road
Belmore NSW 2192
(02) 9759 5242

OTHER STATES

BESTORE ASIAN SUPERMARKET
3/109 Flemington Road
Mitchell ACT 2911
(02) 6241 9595

AJ ASIAN GROCERY
Shop 1/90 Woods Street
Darwin NT 0800
(08) 8981 7955

KOZ MARKET
85 Elizabeth Street
Brisbane QLD 4000
(07) 3220 2677

SEOUL ASIAN GROCERY STORE
66 Grote Street
Adelaide SA 5000
(08) 8212 2755

WING & CO
6 Russell Crescent
Sandy Bay TAS 7005
(03) 6234 5887

KOREA WORLD
4 Ellingworth Parade
Box Hill VIC 3128
(03) 9899 1434

KOREAN KIMCHI GROCERIES
161–163 Brunswick Street
Fitzroy VIC 3065
(03) 9416 3438

KMALL
4/204–208 Bannister Road
Canning Vale WA 6155
(08) 9455 2324

Acknowledgements

PENGUINS

To Julie Gibbs, thank you for giving me the opportunity to share my recipes in this beautiful book that you envisioned so passionately for me.

To Evi O, thank you for the fabulous designs, colours and your imaginative mind in pulling this book together.

To Nicole Abadee, thank you for your patience and skills in helping me edit every word in this book to finally bring it to life, and to Ariane Durkin, Rachel Carter and Anna Scobie, thank you for your invaluable help with this.

To Cassandra Stokes, thank you for your tireless assistance and support in coordinating our team and making everything run effortlessly and smoothly.

To Luisa Brimble, your ability to capture the food I love to eat with your incredible photographic eye and skills will continue to make me smile every time I see your photographs in this book.

To Michelle Noerianto, thank you for your creative stylising touch and constant eye for detail, which has made the feel of each photograph so beautiful.

To the lovely staff at Penguin who have always opened their door to me with a smile and such warmth, thank you.

MY FAMILY

To my mother, Injoung Elshafei, and my father, Mohamed Elshafei, who have taught me the value of food in my life (amongst other life lessons), and have also taught me the importance of preserving their cultural foods in the land we proudly call home.

To my sister, Eman Elshafei, the only and much-loved sister I have been blessed to share life with, whose support has been infinitely invaluable.

To my grandmothers, Amina and Tae Bok, whose treasured influences in cooking have given me inspiration.

Finally, to my friends, whose ever-strengthening friendships have been nothing but appreciated, respected and cherished.

Thank you.

Index

***

A

Adis (Red lentil soup) 65
Alexandrian-style stuffed
    sea bream 112
Atayef (Stuffed pancakes) 176

B

Baba ghanoush 18
Baechu kimchi
    (Pickled cabbage) 71
Baked fish with tahini
    and chilli 97
Bamia (Okra and beef stew) 166
Barbounia fil forn
    (Red mullet with
    tomatoes and onion) 104
Basbousa bi goz el hind
    (Semolina slice with
    coconut) 185
batters
    Skewered beef and
        vegetables 46
    Vegetable bites 39
Bazilla wa lahma (Peas braised
    with meat) 165
beef
    Beef spare rib soup 168
    Bulgogi sliders with kimchi
        mayonnaise 164
    Grilled beef in soy
        marinade 162
    Okra and beef stew 166
    Peas braised with meat 165
    Skewered beef and vegetables
        46
    Steamed kimchi dumplings 42
    Sweet soy sauce-braised beef
        spare ribs 171
Beetroot and yoghurt salad 22
Best chicken soup and
    risoni 126
Bibimpap (Mixed vegetables
    and rice) 78
Bibimguksu (Korean buckwheat
    noodle salad) 72
Biscuits filled with dates
    or pistachios 179
braises
    Braised quince with toasted
        walnut cream 188

Green beans braised in
    olive oil 64
Peas braised with meat 165
Slow-braised baby octopus 94
Slow-braised lamb shanks
    with baby onions and
    dates 156
Sweet soy sauce-braised
    beef spare ribs 171
broad beans
    Egyptian broad bean falafel 60
    Slow-cooked broad beans 63
Bulgogi (Grilled beef in soy
    marinade) 162
Bulgogi sliders with kimchi
    mayonnaise 164

C

carrots
    Moroccan carrots with
        honey, mint and
        cinnamon 50
Charcoaled grey mullet 102
cheese *See* haloumi; labna
chermoula 114
chicken
    Best chicken soup and
        risoni 126
    Chicken kebabs with garlic
        yoghurt 132
    Chicken tagine with
        preserved lemon and green
        olives 138
    Chicken with lamb and
        rice 130
    Egyptian lemon and garlic
        chicken 123
    Harissa chicken 143
    Jute leaves soup 129
    Mum's spicy chicken 136
    My chicken schnitzel 125
    Spicy, sticky Korean chicken
        drumettes 144
    Sweet and sour chicken 140
chickpeas
    Chickpea and tahini dip 24
    Middle Eastern baked eggs 150
Chinese cabbage *See* wombok
Clay-steamed egg 41
couscous
    Jewelled couscous 82

Lamb, prune and fig tagine
    with buttered couscous 152
Quails stuffed with
    couscous 120
crab
    Very hot crab! 92
cucumbers
    Cucumber, mint and
        yoghurt dip 25
    Fattoush 28
    Tayta's salad 26
custards
    Kataifi pastry with milk
        custard 182

D

Dajaj bi laymoon wa toom
    (Egyptian lemon and garlic
    chicken) 123
Dakjjim (Mum's spicy
    chicken) 136
dates
    Biscuits filled with dates
        or pistachios 179
    Slow-braised lamb shanks
        with baby onions and
        dates 156
Deep-fried whitebait 99
dipping sauces
    Kimchi pancakes 36
    Vegetable bites 39
dips
    Baba ghanoush 18
    Chickpea and tahini dip 24
    Cucumber, mint and
        yoghurt dip 25
dressings
    Fattoush 28
    Korean buckwheat
        noodle salad 72
    Mixed vegetables and rice 78
    Tayta's salad 26
    Yang nyum jang dressing 38
    See also vinaigrettes
Dukkah served with labna 49
Dukkah wa labna (Dukkah
    served with labna) 49
dumplings
    Steamed kimchi dumplings 42
Dwangjang chijae (Soy bean
    paste stew) 66

E

eggplants
  Baba ghanoush 18
  Eggplant with cumin
    vinaigrette 29
  Stuffed eggplant and
    zucchini 58
eggs
  Clay-steamed egg 41
  Middle Eastern baked eggs 150
Egyptian broad bean falafel 60
Egyptian lemon and garlic
  chicken 123

F

Fattoush 28
figs
  Halva and fig rounds 194
  Lamb, prune and fig
    tagine with buttered
    couscous 152
fish
  Alexandrian-style stuffed
    sea bream 112
  Baked fish with tahini and
    chilli 97
  Charcoaled grey mullet 102
  Deep-fried whitebait 99
  Mackerel with daikon 111
  Red mullet with tomatoes
    and onion 104
  Sardine kofta tagine 107
  Seafood tagine with
    chermoula 114
  Sumac-crusted trout with
    heirloom tomato salsa 108
Fresh Moroccan mint tea 180
fruits
  Pomegranate and walnut
    salad 31
  Rose petal fruit salad 186
Ful medames (Slow-cooked
  broad beans) 63

G

Galbi tang (Beef spare
  rib soup) 168
Galbijim (Sweet soy sauce-
  braised beef spare ribs) 171
Gambari bi tomb wa filfil harr
  (Garlic and chilli prawns) 90
Garlic and chilli prawns 90
Godungo jorim (Mackerel with
  daikon) 111
Goguma mat-tang (Sweet potato
  with honey) 44
Green beans braised in
  olive oil 64
Grilled beef in soy
  marinade 162

H

haloumi
  String haloumi and
    sumac salad 32

Halva and fig rounds 194
Hamal bi basal wa tamr
  (Slow-braised lamb
  shanks with baby onions
  and dates) 156
Harissa chicken 143
Herb and lemon marinated
  olives 51
Hod-dok (Stuffed sweet fried
  cakes) 193
honey
  Moroccan carrots with
    honey, mint and
    cinnamon 50
  Sweet potato with honey 42
Hummus bi tahina (Chickpea
  and tahini dip) 24

J

Japchae (Stir-fried Korean
  noodles with vegetables) 74
Jewelled couscous 82
Jute leaves soup 129

K

Kataifi pastry with milk
  custard 182
kebabs
  Chicken kebabs with garlic
    yoghurt 132
  Marinated lamb kebabs 155
kimchi
  Bulgogi sliders with kimchi
    mayonnaise 164
  Kimchi pancakes 36
  Pickled cabbage 71
  Steamed kimchi
    dumplings 42
Kimchi bindadok (Kimchi
  pancakes) 36
Kimchi mandu (Steamed
  kimchi dumplings) 42
Korean buckwheat noodle
  salad 72
Korean rice cakes 77
Koshari (Lentil rice) 84
Kufta bi tamatim
  (Middle Eastern meatballs
  in tomato sauce) 158
Kunafa (Kataifi pastry with
  milk custard) 182

L

labna
  Dukkah served with labna 49
lamb
  Chicken with lamb
    and rice 130
  Lamb, prune and fig
    tagine with buttered
    couscous 152
  Marinated lamb kebabs 155
  Middle Eastern meatballs
    in tomato sauce 158
  Savoury lady finger pastries
    with mint yoghurt sauce 52

Slow-braised lamb shanks
  with baby onions and
  dates 156
Za'atar-crusted lamb cutlets
  with rocket salad 161
lemons
  Chicken tagine with
    preserved lemon and green
    olives 138
  Egyptian lemon and garlic
    chicken 123
  Herb and lemon marinated
    olives 51
lentils
  Kimchi pancakes 36
  Lentil rice 84
  Red lentil soup 65
Lubiya bi tamatim wa zeit
  (Green beans braised
  in olive oil) 64

M

Maamoul (Biscuits
  filled with dates or
  pistachios) 179
Mackerel with daikon 111
Mahshi batingan wa kousa
  (Stuffed eggplant and
  zucchini) 58
marinades
  Chicken kebabs with garlic
    yoghurt 132
  Grilled beef in soy
    marinade 162
  Marinated lamb kebabs 155
  Mum's spicy chicken 136
  Skewered beef and
    vegetables 46
Marinated lamb kebabs 155
Middle Eastern baked
  eggs 150
Middle Eastern meatballs
  in tomato sauce 158
mint
  Fresh Moroccan mint
    tea 180
Mixed vegetables and rice 78
Molokhia (Jute leaves soup) 129
Moroccan carrots with
  honey, mint and
  cinnamon 50
Mum's spicy chicken 136
mung beans
  Kimchi pancakes 36
mussels
  Seafood tagine with
    chermoula 114
Muttabal (Baba ghanoush) 18
My chicken schnitzel 125

N

noodles
  Korean buckwheat noodle
    salad 72
  Rice with vermicelli 81
  Stir-fried Korean noodles
    with vegetables 74

nuts
  Biscuits filled with dates
    or pistachios 179
  Braised quince with toasted
    walnut cream 188
  Jewelled couscous 82
  Pomegranate and walnut
    salad 31
  Rice pudding with
    rosewater 190
  Stuffed pancakes 176
  Stuffed sweet fried
    cakes 193
  See also pistachios; walnuts

O
octopus
  Slow-braised baby octopus 94
Ojingoh bokkum (Stir-fried
  squid) 96
Okra and beef stew 166
olives
  Chicken tagine with
    preserved lemon and green
    olives 138
  Herb and lemon marinated
    olives 51
orange blossom syrup 182

P
pancakes
  Kimchi pancakes 36
  Stuffed pancakes 176
Pan-fried tofu with chilli
  and spring onion
  dressing 38
Pasanjeok (Skewered beef
  and vegetables) 46
pastes
  Harissa chicken 143
  Very hot crab! 92
  See also taklia
pastries
  Kataifi pastry with milk
    custard 182
  Savoury lady finger
    pastries with mint yoghurt
    sauce 52
Peas braised with meat 165
Pickled cabbage 71
pistachios
  Biscuits filled with dates or
    pistachios 179
  Stuffed pancakes 176
Pomegranate and walnut
  salad 31
prawns
  Garlic and chilli prawns 90
  Seafood tagine with
    chermoula 114
prunes
  Lamb, prune and fig
    tagine with buttered
    couscous 152
puddings
  Rice pudding with
    rosewater 190

Q
Quails stuffed with
  couscous 120
quinces
  Braised quince with toasted
    walnut cream 188

R
Red lentil soup 65
Red mullet with tomatoes
  and onion 104
rice
  Chicken with lamb and
    rice 130
  Korean rice cakes 77
  Mixed vegetables and
    rice 78
  Rice pudding with
    rosewater 190
  Rice with vermicelli 81
  Saffron rice 83
  Stuffed eggplant and
    zucchini 58
  Stuffed vine leaves 68
Rose petal fruit salad 186
rosewater syrups 176, 185
Roz bi dajaj (Chicken with
  lamb and rice) 130
Roz bi laban (Rice pudding
  with rosewater) 190
Roz bi sha'riyyah (Rice with
  vermicelli) 81
Roz bi za'faran (Saffron rice) 83

S
Safarjal bi qashta wa jooz
  (Braised quince with toasted
  walnut cream) 188
Saffron rice 83
salads
  Beetroot and yoghurt
    salad 22
  Fattoush 28
  Korean buckwheat noodle
    salad 72
  Pomegranate and walnut
    salad 31
  Rose petal fruit salad 186
  String haloumi and sumac
    salad 32
  Sumac-crusted trout
    with heirloom tomato
    salsa 108
  Tayta's salad 26
  Za'atar-crusted lamb cutlets
    with rocket salad 161
Salatah bi rommaan wa jooz
  (Pomegranate and walnut
  salad) 31
Salatah fawakih wa wardah (Rose
  petal fruit salad) 186
Salatah haloumi was summak
  (String haloumi and sumac
  salad) 32
Salwaa wa cuscus (Quails stuffed
  with couscous) 120

Samak bizri bi laymoon
  wa kamoun (Deep-fried
  whitebait) 99
Samak iskandarani
  (Alexandrian-style stuffed
  sea bream) 112
Samak mashwi (Charcoaled grey
  mullet) 102
Samaka harra bi tahina wa filfil
  (Baked fish with tahini and
  chilli) 97
Sardine kofta tagine 107
sauces
  Baked fish with tahini and
    chilli 97
  Egyptian broad bean falafel 60
  Lentil rice 84
  Mackerel with daikon 111
  Middle Eastern meatballs in
    tomato sauce 158
  Red mullet with tomatoes
    and onion 104
  Sardine kofta tagine 107
  Savoury lady finger pastries
    with mint yoghurt sauce 52
  Stir-fried squid 96
  Sweet and sour chicken 140
  Sweet soy sauce-braised beef
    spare ribs 171
sausages
  Middle Eastern baked
    eggs 150
Savoury lady finger pastries
  with mint yoghurt sauce 52
scallops
  Seafood tagine with
    chermoula 114
seafood
  Seafood tagine with
    chermoula 114
  See also crab; fish; octopus;
    mussels; prawns;
    scallops; squid
semolina
  Biscuits filled with dates
    or pistachios 179
  Semolina slice with
    coconut 185
Shakshuka (Middle Eastern
  baked eggs) 150
Shamandr bi zabady (Beetroot
  and yoghurt salad) 22
Shawarma (Marinated lamb
  kebabs) 155
Shay bi na'na (Fresh Moroccan
  mint tea) 180
Shish tawook dajaj wa zabady bi
  toomb (Chicken kebabs with
  garlic yoghurt) 132
Shorbat dajaj bi usfur lisan (Best
  chicken soup and risoni) 126
Skewered beef and vegetables 46
slices
  Semolina slice with
    coconut 185
Slow-braised baby octopus 94
Slow-braised lamb shanks with
  baby onions and dates 156
Slow-cooked broad beans 63

soups
Beef spare rib soup 168
Best chicken soup and
risoni 126
Jute leaves soup 129
Red lentil soup 65
Soy bean paste stew 66
Spicy, sticky Korean chicken
drumettes 144
squid
Stir-fried squid 96
Steamed kimchi dumplings 42
stews
Okra and beef stew 166
Slow-cooked broad beans 63
Soy bean paste stew 66
Stir-fried Korean noodles with
vegetables 74
Stir-fried squid 96
stocks
Chicken with lamb and
rice 130
String haloumi and sumac
salad 32
Stuffed eggplant and
zucchini 58
Stuffed pancakes 176
Stuffed sweet fried cakes 193
Stuffed vine leaves 68
Sumac-crusted trout with
heirloom tomato salsa 108
Sweet and sour chicken 140
Sweet potato with honey 44
sweet potatoes
Sweet potato with honey 44
Vegetable bites 39
Sweet soy sauce-braised beef
spare ribs 171
syrups
Kataifi pastry with milk
custard 182
Semolina slice with
coconut 185
Stuffed pancakes 176

Taamiyah (Egyptian broad
bean falafel) 60
Tagiine bi dajaj bi laymoon
wa zaitoon (Chicken tagine
with preserved lemon
and green olives) 138
Tagiine bi ma'koolat
bahriya wa chermoula
(Seafood tagine with
chermoula) 114
Tagiine bi sardin (Sardine
kofta tagine) 107
tagines
Chicken tagine with
preserved lemon and green
olives 138
Lamb, prune and fig
tagine with buttered
couscous 152
Sardine kofta tagine 107
Seafood tagine with
chermoula 114

tahini
Baked fish with tahini
and chilli 97
Chickpea and tahini dip 24
Egyptian broad bean
falafel 60
taklia 166
Tang su yeok (Sweet and sour
chicken) 140
Tayta's salad 26
tea
Fresh Moroccan mint tea 180
tofu
Pan-fried tofu with chilli and
spring onion dressing 38
tomatoes
Lentil rice 84
Middle Eastern meatballs in
tomato sauce 158
Sumac-crusted trout with
heirloom tomato salsa 108
Tteokbokki (Korean rice cakes) 77
Tubu buchim (Pan-fried tofu
with chilli and spring onion
dressing) 38
Tukbaegi gaeranjim
(Clay-steamed egg) 41

Ukhtubut bi tamatim
(Slow-braised baby
octopus) 94

vegetables
Beetroot and yoghurt
salad 22
Eggplant with cumin
vinaigrette 29
Fattoush 28
Green beans braised in
olive oil 64
Jute leaves soup 129
Korean buckwheat noodle
salad 72
Korean rice cakes 77
Mackerel with daikon 111
Mixed vegetables and rice 78
Moroccan carrots with
honey, mint and
cinnamon 50
Okra and beef stew 166
Peas braised with meat 165
Pickled cabbage 71
Skewered beef and
vegetables 46
Soy bean paste stew 66
Stir-fried Korean noodles
with vegetables 74
Stuffed eggplant and
zucchini 58
Sumac-crusted trout with
heirloom tomato salsa 108
Sweet potato with honey 42
Tayta's salad 26
Vegetable bites 39
Very hot crab! 92

vinaigrette
Eggplant with cumin
vinaigrette 29
vine leaves
Stuffed vine leaves 68

walnuts
Braised quince with toasted
walnut cream 188
Pomegranate and
walnut salad 31
Stuffed pancakes 176
Wara einab (Stuffed vine
leaves) 68
wombok
Pickled cabbage 71

Yacha tigim (Vegetable bites) 39
yoghurt
Beetroot and yoghurt salad 22
Chicken kebabs with garlic
yoghurt 132
Cucumber, mint and yoghurt
dip 25
Marinated lamb kebabs 155
Savoury lady finger
pastries with mint yoghurt
sauce 52

Za'atar-crusted lamb cutlets
with rocket salad 161
Zabady bi khiyar wa na'naa
(Cucumber, mint and yoghurt
dip) 25
Zaitoun bi 'ashab (Herb and
lemon marinated olives) 51
zucchini
Stuffed eggplant and
zucchini 58

LANTERN

Published by the Penguin Group
Penguin Group (Australia)
707 Collins Street, Melbourne, Victoria 3008, Australia
(a division of Penguin Australia Pty Ltd)
Penguin Group (USA) Inc.
375 Hudson Street, New York, New York 10014, USA
Penguin Group (Canada)
90 Eglinton Avenue East, Suite 700, Toronto,
Canada ON M4P 2Y3
(a division of Penguin Canada Books Inc.)
Penguin Books Ltd
80 Strand, London WC2R 0RL England
Penguin Ireland
25 St Stephen's Green, Dublin 2, Ireland
(a division of Penguin Books Ltd)
Penguin Books India Pvt Ltd
11 Community Centre, Panchsheel Park,
New Delhi – 110 017, India
Penguin Group (NZ)
67 Apollo Drive, Rosedale, Auckland 0632, New Zealand
(a division of Penguin New Zealand Pty Ltd)
Penguin Books (South Africa) (Pty) Ltd, Rosebank Office
Park, Block D, 181 Jan Smuts Avenue, Parktown North,
Johannesburg, 2196, South Africa
Penguin (Beijing) Ltd
7F, Tower B, Jiaming Center, 27 East Third Ring Road
North, Chaoyang District, Beijing 100020, China

Penguin Books Ltd, Registered Offices:
80 Strand, London, WC2R 0RL, England

First published by Penguin Group (Australia), 2015

10 9 8 7 6 5 4 3 2 1

Design by Evi O. © Penguin Group (Australia)
Pattern illustrations by Evi O. and Hannah Schubert
Food styling by Michelle Noerianto
Typeset in Caecilia by Post Pre-press Group,
Brisbane, Queensland
Colour separation by Splitting Image Colour Studio,
Clayton, Victoria
Printed and bound in China by C & C Offset Printing Co Ltd

National Library of Australia
Cataloguing-in-Publication data:

Elshafei, Amina, author.
Amina's home cooking / Amina Elshafei;
Luisa Brimble, photographer.
ISBN: 9780143797739 (paperback)
Includes index.
Cooking.
Other Authors/Contributors:
Brimble, Luisa, photographer.

641.5

penguin.com.au/lantern